On Iowa

A University and Its People

The Gothic tower of the hospital at night. *1962 photograph by UI Photographic Service.*

Contents

On the cover:
"There it stands—the Old Stone Capitol—a work of art, radiating the spiritual values of simplicity and dignity, proportion and harmony, poise and tranquillity."
—*B.F. Shambaugh,*
The Old Stone Capitol Remembers
Reprinted by permission of the Iowa State Historical Department/Office of the State Historical Society. *Photograph by Joan Liffring-Zug.*

Inside front cover: This graceful, handsome staircase greets the visitor entering Old Capitol from the east portico. The staircase was installed during the 1921-24 renovation, replacing the original with only minor changes in design. It was extended to the ground floor at that time. Since it veers to the left at the bottom, it is a reverse spiral. In most such staircases the first curve is to the right. Another unusual feature is that the top step is directly above the bottom step. No two of the 103 balusters supporting the handrail are the same height. The steps are of oak and the banisters and handrail are walnut. *Photograph by Gary Jones.*

Acknowledgments

We would like to thank especially Earl Rogers, director of the University Archives, for his assistance. He has the whole history of the University filed away in his head and was most generous in sharing it with us.

Our thanks go to recipe contributors; editors of *Old Capitol Cookbook*; Dean Borg, Thomas E. Brown, Jo-Ann Conklin, Larry Eckholt, Phil Haddy, Phillip E. Jones, Margaret Keyes, Don McQuillen, Debra Neal, Mary Parden, Gordon Strayer, Alan Swanson, Bette Thompson, the Audiovisual Center and the Office of Public Information, The University of Iowa; Al Grady, Jane Gray, Edwin B. Green and Irving B. Weber, Iowa City; and Ruth Julin, Monticello, Iowa.

Dedication

This book is dedicated with love to my parents, Lola and Walter Johnston of Marshalltown, Iowa, who, among other kindnesses, supported me with their faith and their checkbook while I was a student at The University of Iowa.

About the Author

Louise Roalson graduated from The University of Iowa in 1946 with a B.A. degree in journalism. She is a member of Theta Sigma Phi, honorary professional journalism fraternity, Kappa Tau Alpha, honorary journalism scholastic fraternity, and Phi Beta Kappa.

She was a reporter on the *Daily Iowan*, the *Marshalltown Times-Republican* and the *Cedar Rapids Gazette*. A free-lance writer and editor, she compiled the prize-winning *Notably Norwegian*, a book of ethnic recipes and folk art published in 1982 by Penfield Press of Iowa City.

Her husband, John, is a dentist and also a UI graduate. Mrs. Roalson is a member of Delta Delta Delta sorority. Dr. Roalson is a member of Delta Sigma Delta professional fraternity. They have three sons and live in Cedar Rapids, Iowa.

The Roalsons are life members of the Iowa Alumni Association.

Honorary Degree (1937), lithograph by Grant Wood. On loan to The University of Iowa Museum of Art. Grant Wood, center, caricatured himself as pudgy and cherubic between two gaunt scholars, posed by Dean Emeritus Carl E. Seashore, right, of the Graduate College, and Prof. Norman Foerster, left, director of the School of Letters of The University of Iowa. Wood was the recipient of four honorary degrees. *University of Iowa Museum of Art. Anonymous loan.*

Photography: Lloyd Bender, Esther Feske, A. Drake Hokanson, Gary Jones, Tom Jorgensen, Fred Kent, Jim Kent, Joan Liffring-Zug, Don Roberts, Marc Schultz and Charles Seemuth.
Graphic Design: Esther Feske
Recipe Consultant: Miriam Canter
Editors: John Zug, Nancy McHugh
Typesetting: Mary Vaughn
Printed by Julin Printing Co., Monticello, Iowa

ISBN 0-941016-13-7
Library of Congress Catalog Number 83-62320
Copyright 1983 Penfield Press

Published by Penfield Press
215 Brown Street
Iowa City, Iowa 52240 U.S.A.

No Place Like It

Framed by cornfields, The University of Iowa is a microcosm—a miniature world where you can find whatever you seek. For some, it's an ivory tower of thought, study and scholarly research. For others, it's a penny arcade of fun and games; for still others, a perpetual arts festival that delights the soul.

A fantastic potpourri of people and ideas, it has a deserved reputation as "The Athens of the Midwest." It's a unique combination of a massive hospital complex, Big Ten sports scene and a cultural center, a strange medley that somehow works —and seems right.

It's a place where Paul Engle writes poetry, James Van Allen explores space, where novels are written and space satellites built, where Arab shieks fly in for eye surgery, where Grant Wood painted his cotton-ball trees, and the late great Dr. Arthur Steindler gained fame as a mender of hobbled limbs.

There's no place in Iowa like Iowa City, maybe no place anywhere. It's exciting, dramatic and more than slightly kooky.

Where else would a young lawyer who doubles as a juggler run for Pope? Where else would a poet pseudonymed Dr. Alphabet write poetry around a city block? Where else would a bank teller get held up in broad daylight by a guy wearing rubber fins and a snorkeling mask who walks out onto the street and is swallowed up in the crowd?

Eclectic in all things, the UI is an architectural textbook illustrated in three dimensions. You'll find Greek columns, Gothic towers, gables, gargoyles, cupolas and parapets. (If it looks like a castle, it's probably a fraternity house.)

Iowa City is a company town, and the University is the company. It's Iowa City's biggest employer (17,000), and it spills $26 million a month into Iowa City's economy.

Students enroll at UI from all over the world. If everyone on campus spoke in native dialect, it would be the Tower of Babel. A freshman coed from What Cheer, Iowa, can get her first glimpse of a turbaned Sikh (but, like her, he may be wearing blue jeans).

The UI turns out doctors, accountants, dentists, nurses, lawyers, engineers, teachers, artists, novelists, actors, musicians—and more.

There's no better place to be than Iowa City on a crisp fall day when the trees in front of Old Capitol turn gold and red, there's a nip in the air and the Iowa River flows peacefully through the heart of the campus.

This little book with its facts and figures, its recipes and history, is an introduction to the University for some and a nostalgic remembrance of things past for others.

Iowa All the Way

The University of Iowa was named for Iowa the state, which was named for Iowa the territory, which was named for Iowa the river, and where the river got its name, we don't know. It could have been from the Ioway Indians. The usual translation of "Iowa" from Indian is "this is the place" or "beautiful land." *Webster's New World Dictionary*, however, translates it as "sleepy ones: a scornful appellation." What would Webster know about it?

An Old Nickname

The Hawkeye nickname in Iowa dates back to territorial days. It comes from the name given to Natty Bumppo, a white scout, by Indians in James Fenimore Cooper's 1826 novel, *The Last of the Mohicans*. Even before Iowa became a state, citizens in Iowa Territory referred to themselves as Hawkeyes. The Territorial Legislature made it official, as the state did later, and eventually, the University. Two Burlington men, Judge David Rorer and James G. Edwards, were credited with popularizing the nickname. Edwards called his newspaper the *Burlington Hawk-Eye*.

A hawk was depicted on the great seal of the Territory of Iowa.

Facts and Figures

Founded: Feb. 25, 1847
Iowa City, Iowa
Enrollment: approximately 30,000
Faculty: more than 1,600
Campus: 1,880 acres (central campus, 900 acres)
Buildings: 90 major, countless smaller ones
University Libraries: more than 2 million volumes
Ten Colleges: Liberal Arts, Business Administration, Medicine, Engineering, Law, Nursing, Pharmacy, Dentistry, Education, and the Graduate College
Seven Schools: Art and Art History, Journalism and Mass Communication, Letters, Library Science, Music, Religion, and Social Work
Number of degrees conferred: over 175,000
Living alumni: over 130,000
Professional fraternities: 6
Undergraduate social fraternities: 23
National sororities: 18
Residence halls: 11 (5 on east campus and 6 on west campus)
Governing body: State Board of Regents
Nickname: Hawkeyes
Colors: black and old gold

Old Gold

For 33 years the University went without school colors. In the spring of 1887 fifty seniors met on the steps of Old Capitol and voted, not for just gold, but for "old gold." Legend has it that a coed wearing an old gold scarf tore it to bits, and each student left the meeting with a scrap of Old Gold pinned to his or her lapel. Where the black comes from nobody seems to know. If the gold represents ripening grain (one theory), perhaps the black symbolizes Iowa's rich soil.

Presidents of
The University of Iowa

James O. Freedman 1982-present
Willard L. Boyd, Jr. 1969-81
Howard R. Bowen 1964-69
Virgil M. Hancher 1940-64
Eugene A. Gilmore 1934-40
Walter A. Jessup 1916-34
Thomas H. Macbride 1914-16
John G. Bowman 1911-14
George E. MacLean 1899-1911
Charles A. Schaeffer 1887-98
Josiah L. Pickard 1878-87
George J. Thacher 1871-77
James Black 1868-70
Oliver M. Spencer 1862-67
Silas Totten 1859-62
Amos Dean 1855-59

Acting presidents: Duane C. Spriestersbach (1981-82), Chester A. Phillips (1940), Amos N. Currier (1898-99), Christian W. Slagle (1877-78) and Nathan Leonard (1867-68 and 1870-71).

What's in a Name?

If you continue to think of the University as "SUI," you are suffering from a mild case of nostalgia. In 1959, Iowa State College in Ames changed its name to Iowa State University, so for a while there was an SUI and an ISU. Confusion reigned. In 1964, the State University of Iowa dropped "State" from its name, except in legal contracts. To further befuddle you, be advised that SUI/UI called itself "Iowa State University" from 1866 to 1875. Today it's "The University of Iowa"—or the more popular "UI." But it would take an amendment to the state constitution to make it "really official."

Around Iowa City

On the Campus:

Old Capitol—First capitol of Iowa. Open for tours Monday through Saturday 10 a.m.-3 p.m., Sunday noon - 4 p.m.; Saturdays of home football games 9 a.m.-noon.

Museum of Natural History—Macbride Hall northeast of Old Capitol. Specimens of bird and animal life and artifacts from other cultures. Iowa Hall (1984) features Iowa's natural history. Monday through Saturday 8:00 a.m.-5:00 p.m., Sunday 12:30-4:30 p.m.

Museum of Art—The Owen and Leone Elliott Collections, University permanent collection and visiting shows. Open Tuesday-Saturday 10 a.m.-5 p.m., Sunday noon-5 p.m. Tours available. Closed Monday.

Hancher Auditorium—One of the nation's finest major multipurpose theaters. Tours Wednesdays and Sundays at 2 p.m. from box office when University in session, 353-6251.

Campus Tours—Student guides available when University in session from Office of Admissions, 108 Calvin Hall, weekdays at 10:30 and 2:30 and Saturdays at 11 a.m. Group tours call Office of Public Information, 5 Old Capitol, 353-5691.

Dining for campus visitors—River Room cafeteria, State Room restaurant (lunches only) or Union Station snack bar, all in Iowa Memorial Union; the Quadrangle cafeteria or the General Hospital coffee shop.

Off the Campus:

"Old Brick" at the corner of Clinton and Market Streets—The oldest church building in Iowa City. Built from 1856-1865, formerly the home of the First Presbyterian Church, came close to being demolished in 1977, but admirers saved it. Now on National Register of Historic Places.

Plum Grove—Restored home of Robert Lucas, first governor of the Territory of Iowa, built in 1844. Located at 1030 Carroll Street, off Kirkwood Avenue. Open Wednesday through Sunday, 1-5 p.m., April through November.

Summit Street Homes—Residential area of Victorian-style homes built from 1860 to 1910. Houses number 301 to 818 between Burlington Street and the railroad overpass. On the National Register of Historic Places. Exterior viewing only. Don't miss the "Gingerbread House" at the corner of College and Summit.

Mormon Handcart Historical Site—Four-acre site west of Mormon Trek Road, from which 2,400 immigrants began a 1,400-mile journey by foot to Utah in 1856-57.

Downtown Iowa City:

Old Capitol Shopping Mall across Washington Street from Schaeffer Hall.

Pedestrian Mall (College Street between Clinton and Linn).

Long-time campus bars, Joe's Place and the Airliner.

(Whetstone's Drug Store at Washington and Clinton is no more, alas.)

Near Iowa City:

Hoover Memorial—West Branch, 10 miles east of Iowa City on I-80. Herbert Hoover's birthplace cottage and gravesite and the Presidential Museum and Library. Open 8 a.m.-6 p.m. weekdays and 10 a.m.-6 p.m. Sundays Memorial Day to Labor Day. Sept.-May: 9-5 weekdays, 12-5 Sundays.

Coralville Reservoir and Lake Macbride State Park—5 miles north of Iowa City. Recreational area for fishing, hunting, camping, swimming, boating and waterskiing.

Amana Colonies—Seven villages founded in 1854, communal until 1932. Twenty miles west of Iowa City on Highway 6. Old-world crafts and German foods.

Cedar Rapids—Iowa's second largest city is 25 miles north on I-380.

Kalona—Horse-and-buggy Old Order Amish, the more liberal Mennonites and restaurants serving traditional foods. On Highway 1, 18 miles south of Iowa City. Tours available from the Kalona Historical Society, Box 292, Kalona, Iowa 52247.

A Short Course in UI History

1838

This is still Indian country. Mesquakies roam current site of UI campus. Chief Powesheik gives farewell speech July 4 as tribe prepares to move west.

1840

Cornerstone for Old Capitol laid, building occupied in 1842 by Territory of Iowa government.

Feb. 25, 1847

State University of Iowa founded by First General Assembly in Old Capitol, just two months after Iowa becomes a state. U.S. government gives state 46,080 acres of land to be sold for University funds. UI becomes the 17th state university and second west of the Mississippi. Lack of funds keeps University from opening for eight years.

March 1855

First term of 16 weeks: tuition $4, two professors, "about 40" students. First state university to admit women on equal basis.

September 1855

Amos Dean so casual about being first president he stays in Albany, N.Y., where he is chancellor of a law school. Visits Iowa City only three times during his tenure, 1855-59. Told he must move to Iowa City, he promptly resigns.

Classes held in rented Mechanics Academy, present site of Seashore Hall, only building used until 1858.

1856-57

Nine departments plus Normal Department (a teachers' college) and a Preparatory Department for preparing students to attend the University since state has few high schools.

UI has no campus, owns no buildings.

First catalog shows 124 students (83 men, 41 women). Only 19 in Collegiate Department, rest in Normal and Preparatory departments.

1857

Capital of Iowa moved from Iowa City to Des Moines. Iowa City loses capital but retains University. State gives University Old Capitol and 10 acres of land.

State Historical Society founded, housed in Old Capitol.

One of the earliest photographs of Old Capitol was taken at the Johnson County Fair of 1853. This view from the southeast shows the building before the east portico was in place. In the foreground is a team of four oxen pulling a wagon.

1858

Class of 1858 has one graduate—Dexter Edson Smith. It will be five years before the next diploma is granted.

Museum of Natural History founded.

State Legislature makes first appropriation to UI—$13,000 for new buildings and repairs. Many think no need for state to support UI.

1858-60

University closes for two years because of money problems. Normal Department stays open.

1860

UI reopens with five professors, 172 students and President Silas Totten, who introduces idea of research.

1862

Horses, cows and pigs ramble freely on the grounds of Old Capitol. UI tells janitor, who lives in basement of Old Capitol, to buy a dog for five dollars or less to help him keep livestock off campus.

Civil War takes most men from campus; 124 enlist.

1863

South Hall, first UI building after Old Capitol. (Burned 1901.)

1864

UI begins receiving regular biennial appropriations from State Legislature. Bill passed in 1878 guarantees annual funding.

1865

Civil War vets can enroll free if enlistees; by 1866, draftees also and, in 1867, orphans of veterans.

1866

North Hall built (burned in 1897, demolished 1949).

Mechanics Academy acquired (built 1843, demolished 1897).

1867

Alumni Association established.

1868

Law School established, first west of Mississippi, moved to UI from Des Moines, where it was founded in 1865. Classes in House Chamber of Old Capitol until 1910.

Prof. Gustavus Hinrichs builds chemistry lab, said to be one of best in country. Internationally known for his research and use of the scientific method, he founds the Iowa Weather Service (forerunner of the State Weather Bureau), first state weather service in U.S.

The Price Was Right

"Good board may be obtained in respectable families at from two dollars to two-fifty per week." It said so in the first circular of the University, Sept. 1, 1855.

The Women Won

The question: Would women be permitted to enroll in the UI when it reopened in 1860 after a two-year closing due to lack of funds? On April 28, 1858, the Board of Trustees said no. Heated debate followed. Women's minds were "inferior," said some. It was all right for women to attend lectures, but not as students, said others. Women would distract male students. The last word came from the faculty, who assured the trustees that women students could handle the work and would not be a bad influence.

Party Time!

In the 1860s students would gather for a social event called a "walkaround." The sexes mingled in a room at Old Capitol. A young man would ask a young woman to walk with him, and the couple would march around the entire room. Period.

One of Those Days

Mark Twain definitely did *not* "have a good day" when he lectured in Iowa City in 1867. He found the Clinton Hotel "shabby and disagreeable," the clerk woke him at 6 a.m. instead of 10 o'clock, and he suffered a bruised hip when he fell while boarding an omnibus headed for the railroad depot.

1870

Medical School established.

1872

First permanent college-level department of education in U.S. established.

Normal Department (teacher training) closes.

1873

Mechanics Academy remodeled into 20-bed hospital for training medical students, co-administered with Sisters of Mercy.

1874

Observatory built where President's House now stands.

Department of Military Science and Training established.

1878

Phoebe W. Sudlow of English Department first woman professor.

1879

Preparatory Department closes; state high schools charged with preparing students for higher education. One prep school is called Iowa City Academy.

1882

Dental School, first west of the Mississippi, established.

1883

Prof. Hinrichs, brilliant but controversial, dismissed amid long classical-scientific battle.

1884

Science Hall built on present site of Macbride Hall, renamed Calvin Hall for Samuel Calvin, professor in the Department of Geology, 1873-1911.

1885

Department of Pharmacy established.

Electives permitted for first time.

1890

Hall of Pharmacy and Chemistry erected, becomes a library in 1924, Electrical Engineering Building in 1930; renamed East Hall Annex in 1966. (Demolished 1973.)

1892

Summer School classes begin; professors paid according to number of students per class. Plan fails, but in 1899 state begins funding summer sessions.

Semester-hour system starts, a revolutionary idea that a student need attend each class only three times a week.

They Cleaned Up Their Act

Classes were dismissed one fine spring day in 1869 so that students and faculty could clean up the campus (except for law students, who exercised their constitutional rights and voted not to). The students removed dead trees, trimmed walks, made new paths, dug around the trees and removed stones. Then it was lemonade for everybody, and a group picture was taken. The student newspaper, the *Reporter*, said: "The evening was spent in strolling about, playing croquet and other innocent sports, until by mutual consent the company dispersed, all feeling tired bodily, but rested mentally, and all well pleased with the work done and the greatly improved appearance of the campus."

Class-y Gifts

The Class of 1865 planted trees around the campus, a tradition for class gifts through the 1860s. The graduating class of 1870 broke tradition, presenting the University with a 6,650-pound boulder from a bluff outside town. It still sits in in front of Schaeffer Hall. Balancing it on the Macbride side of Old Capitol is a boulder from the Class of 1880.

Top Score

In 1872, the sophomore class challenged the rest of the University to a baseball game and lost, 45-22. The sophs treated the victors to an oyster supper. In 1876, a baseball team was organized and played a game against Cornell College—the beginning of intercollegiate sports at UI.

1894

(Old) Dental Building erected. (Part removed 1923, demolished 1975.)

(Old) Iowa Field acquired for football, track and baseball.

1895

Phi Beta Kappa chartered.

1896

World's first official basketball game played with five men on a team in Close Hall, Iowa vs. Chicago. Previously, teams had nine players.

1897

University Hospital, first one operated by state, built on location of Mechanics Hall, later named East Hall, renamed Seashore Hall for Carl. E. Seashore, head of the Department of Psychology, 1905-42, and of the Graduate School, 1908-36 and 1942-46.

1898

School of Nursing established.

1899

UI admitted to Western Intercollegiate Conference (Big 10).

1900

First extension class.

Bertha Belle Quaintance named first registrar.

School of Political and Social Science, College of Liberal Arts, Department of Physical Education and Athletics, and Graduate College established.

First Ph.D. awarded to Fred D. Merritt for his study on Iowa banking.

Department of Pharmacy becomes College of Pharmacy.

1901

Alice Young first dean of women.

1902

Collegiate Building built, later called Hall of Liberal Arts, renamed Schaeffer Hall for Charles A. Schaeffer, UI president, 1887-98.

1903

Engineering Department becomes School of Applied Science and, in 1905, College of Applied Science.

1904

(Old) Armory and Men's Gymnasium and Zoology Building erected. Men's Gym is setting for University parties before Memorial Union built.

Tuition $20 a year.

Enrollment 1,560.

A University football game on Old Iowa Field, probably between 1894 and 1901. Buildings on the skyline are South Hall, with many chimneys, and Old Medical Building, both south of Old Capitol on what later became the Pentacrest.

1905

UI moves Calvin Hall (6,000 tons) across Jefferson Street to present location, Capitol and Jefferson. Project takes all summer, progressing two feet a day. Clears way for President MacLean's plan for Pentacrest. Classes continue during move; not even a test tube upset.

Engineering Building constructed.

1906

Department of Fine Arts established.

1907

Enrollment 2,000.

Department of Education becomes School of Education.

William Howard Taft, secretary of war (and later President of the U.S.), gives Commencement address.

1908

Hall of Natural Science built, later renamed Macbride Hall for Thomas H. Macbride, professor of botany, 1878-1914, and UI president, 1914-16.

President's House built for $25,000.

1909

UI elected to Association of American Universities.

Iowa Lakeside Laboratory established at Lake Okoboji so students can study geology, botany and aquatic biology during summer sessions.

1910

College of Law Building erected, called North Hall, 1962-64, renamed Gilmore Hall for Eugene A. Gilmore, professor in College of Law, 1929-52, and dean, 1929-34; UI president, 1934-40.

Department of Physics begins work with radioactivity.

1911

Forest C. Ensign first dean of men.

1912

First student union in Unitarian Church Building.

10-watt Station 9YA, forerunner of WSUI (campus radio station), receives experimental license from U.S. Department of Commerce.

Physics Building erected; fourth building of Pentacrest. From 1966 to 1969, called Mathematical Sciences Building. Renamed MacLean Hall for George E. MacLean, UI president, 1899-1911.

First Homecoming celebration.

1913

Home Economics Department and Extension Division (now Division of Continuing Education) established.

It Takes Two

Students in the early 1900s were gaga over the tango, but it was condemned by the faculty. Perhaps it was the gypsy origins of the dance or the Latin beat of the music or the cheek-to-cheek stance that flustered the elders.

Scantily Clad?

In 1908 the lively head of the Women's Physical Education Department, Alice Wilkinson (Bates), chose bloomers and "low-necked" blouses for her students to wear in a public athletic exhibition. A few students rebelled, enlisting the help of the dean of women. Miss Wilkinson threatened to resign if the uniforms were not worn, asserting that young women should not become overly modest.

A compromise was reached. Tickets were given to each participant, who could give them to whomever she chose, thus restricting the audience.

Pictures of those controversial outfits show yards and yards of material in the bloomers, and no way would the necklines be called low by today's standards.

'The Greatest'

Iowa City heard at 3 a.m. about the Armistice ending World War I Nov. 11, 1918. A wild celebration ensued with dancing in the streets, fireworks and a parade (the Currier Hall girls contributed a "comb orchestra"). University classes were called off for the day. Since the SATC boys (Student Army Training Corps) could not leave campus, there was an all-day dance in Liberal Arts Hall (now Schaeffer Hall). Local observers of many freewheeling celebrations say this was the greatest ever. After all, it was "the war to end *all* wars."

School of Education becomes College of Education.

Currier Hall, women's dormitory, built, first residence hall, houses 170 women. Named for Amos N. Currier, professor in the Latin Department, 1866-98, and acting president, 1898-99.

Five-Mile Act becomes law, outlawing liquor within a five-mile radius of campus.

1914

School of Commerce established.

Eastlawn built as nurses' residence.

1915

Course offered in "Political and Legal Status of Women."

Women's Gymnasium built, renamed Halsey Gymnasium for Elizabeth Halsey, head of Physical Education for Women, 1927-56.

Department of Music and Department of Art established.

1916

Enrollment 3,523.

(Old) Music Building erected.

University High School established (closed 1972).

1917

Department of Music becomes School of Music.

Dental Building constructed, renamed Trowbridge Hall for Arthur Trowbridge, head of Department of Geology, 1934-52.

Opening of Iowa Child Welfare Research Station, world's first center to study normal child (later Institute of Child Behavior and Development).

World War I depletes ranks of male faculty and students. Some 1,500 serve in the armed forces; 41 are killed.

1918

Flu epidemic hits 1,000 students, faculty and townspeople. University quarantined for two months, bringing school to virtual standstill. In Iowa City, many die.

1919

ROTC (Reserve Officers' Training Corps) begins, compulsory until 1963.

Children's Hospital built, referred to as "Perkins' Hospital" after Eli C. Perkins, state legislator who sponsored a bill providing free care for sick and crippled indigent children, renamed Steindler Building in 1983 for Dr. Arthur Steindler, founder and head of the Department of Orthopedic Surgery, 1927-52.

Eastlawn, home of nurses, School of Music and now offices.

1920s

Sororities and fraternities begin, replacing literary societies which flourished from about 1860 to 1920.

1920

Quadrangle Dormitory for men occupied, first building on west campus. Built as military barracks but WW I ended before completion.

Enrollment 5,395.

1921-24

Old Capitol remodeled.

1921

Westlawn Nurses Home, the Armory and Psychopathic Hospital (now Psychiatric Hospital) built.

World's first pre-school laboratory established.

School of Commerce becomes College of Commerce (now College of Business Administration).

1922

WSUI begins operation, first educational radio station west of the Mississippi.

UI pioneers in accepting creative writing or art in lieu of thesis for advanced degree.

1924

University Hall, final building in the Pentacrest, erected, renamed Jessup Hall for Walter A. Jessup, dean of the College of Education, 1912-16, and UI president, 1916-34.

Brothers W.O. and E.C. Finkbine give 17 acres of land west of the campus for golf course.

Department of Journalism established.

Close Hall acquired (built 1891, damaged by fire 1940, demolished 1968), named for Helen S. Close, major contributor. Used for YMCA and YWCA and later for journalism classes and the *Daily Iowan*.

Chemistry-Botany Building erected.

1925

University Schools, observational school for College of Education, built, renamed North Hall in 1973, the third building in UI history to be so called.

Quadrangle doubled in size (700 men residents).

School of Religion established, first in a state university.

1926

Medical Laboratories and first unit of Iowa Memorial Union constructed.

Department of Journalism becomes School of Journalism.

A spring festival on the Pentacrest, circa 1920.

Taking the Pledge

"I pledge, here and now, a life-long loyalty to the ideals of scholarship and character of the founders of this institution to the end that I may loyally serve the University, the Commonwealth, and this Nation." This was the pledge first recited by new students at the University Induction Ceremony on the west terrace of Old Capitol at 8 a.m. Oct. 4, 1921. The band played "Old Gold," a prayer was read, President Jessup gave a welcome and everyone sang "America." Similar rituals were followed at the beginning of each fall term until 1968, when such pomp fell into disfavor with the young.

Mencken's View

In 1925, H.L. Mencken wrote in *American Mercury* magazine, "Iowa City is now the literary capital of the United States."

1927

Field House dedicated (considered largest and best of any university in the country).

Addition to Currier Hall built.

1928

General Hospital dedicated. Building costs $5 million, half paid by Rockefeller grant, half by state.

Power Plant erected.

1929

School of Fine Arts and School of Letters established.

Iowa Stadium dedicated, renamed Kinnick Stadium in 1972 in honor of Nile Kinnick, famed halfback on the 1939 Ironmen football team.

1931

Iowa Institute of Hydraulic Research established, one of foremost research centers of its type in the world.

Mechanical Engineering Laboratory built.

1932-39

UI's W9XK, world's first educational TV station to operate on a regular basis. UI experimenting in TV since 1923.

1933

Hydraulics Laboratory built.

1935

Law Commons constructed.

Nuclear research begins.

1936

Writers' Workshop created.

Art Building and University Theatre erected.

1938

Hillcrest Dormitory built.

1940

WSUI radio station increases power from 1,000 to 5,000 watts.

1942

Dean of Men's Office, Dean of Women's Office and Employment Service merge into Office of Student Affairs under C. Woody Thompson.

South Quadrangle dormitory built by the Navy.

1942-45

Most male students off to World War II. Campus facilities used by military programs—Navy Pre-Flight School, Navy Aviation Training Program, Army Specialized Training Program and programs for both Army and Navy medical and dental students. A total of 36,357 military personnel trains at UI.

Iowa City Gothic

Grant Wood, Iowa's most widely known artist, bought, restored and lived in the house at 1142 East Court Street. Dressed in his beloved bib overalls, he did much of the work himself. The house, built in 1858 by Nicholas Oaks, is now the home of lawyer James P. Hayes. It still has its original picket fence. Wood was on the art faculty from 1934 until his death in 1942.

No Cruelty

The Society for Prevention of Cruelty to After-Dinner Speakers was a fun group of the 1930s, founded and guided by Grant Wood, Frank Luther Mott and others. They lured nationally known speakers to Iowa City and entertained them in Victorian-decorated quarters above Roland Smith's cafe.

Sacred Cow Kicked

Acerbic architect Frank Lloyd Wright left Iowa Citians fuming after his on-campus lecture in 1939. He pooh-poohed *all* of the city's buildings, singling out Old Capitol for special scorn as being *most* inappropriate to its time and place. He also told the students they were on "a four-year loaf."

The Mayflower

Once upon a time there was a fine mansion where the Mayflower Residence Hall (formerly the Mayflower Apartments) now stands. In the 1920s and 1930s, it was turned into a restaurant, the Red Ball Inn. Called the Mayflower during the 1940s, the converted mansion was a popular student drinking and dancing spot. Pre-flight cadets were so fond of it that they referred to it as their "club."

1945-46

Influx of male students on GI Bill, which pays tuition, supplies and subsistence allowance. University sets up temporary quonset hut villages—Templin, Westlawn, Riverside, Stadium and Finkbine parks—to house veterans and their families. Enrollment jumps from 4,714 in 1945 to 9,770 in 1946.

1948

Enrollment 10,862.

School of Social Work added to College of Liberal Arts.

Ten-ton atom smasher added to Department of Physics.

Institute of Public Affairs established, providing information and services to city, county and state governments and to citizen groups.

School of Nursing becomes College of Nursing.

1951

Communications Center (Journalism) and Main Library built.

1952

Enrollment dips to 7,213, then steadily increases. Veterans Administration Hospital erected.

1953

Danforth Chapel built next to Iowa Memorial Union, named for William H. Danforth, major contributor.

Dental Hygiene program established.

1954

University Hospital School constructed.

New Finkbine golf course built.

1955

Institute of Agricultural Medicine established on Oakdale campus, first in Western Hemisphere.

Second unit of Iowa Memorial Union built.

Parklawn Apartments (married housing) built.

1956

University of Iowa Foundation established to raise funds for the University through gifts and bequests.

1957

Medical Research Center erected.

Audiology added to Department of Speech Pathology.

'Swing and Sway the Crandic Way'

Before so many students owned cars, the CRANDIC (Cedar Rapids and Iowa City) interurban was a popular way for students to make the 27-mile trip between the two cities. For 49 years, beginning in 1904, the "Vomit Comet," as the students fondly called it, hurtled its way along the winding track to "C.R." The Iowa City depot was at College and Clinton Streets, and the Cedar Rapids depot, downtown at Fourth Avenue and Third Street. The last passenger run was on May 30, 1953, when 300 nostalgic citizens took a ritualistic farewell round trip. Cedar Rapids was once the place for UI students to head for non-campus night life. Danceland Ballroom and the Yacht Club, both now gone, were popular in yesteryear.

Good Connections

Good railroad connections with Chicago enabled Iowa City to attract illustrious speakers in bygone days. Chicago was one of the main stops on the speaking circuit.

Some of those celebrities were Mark Twain, Horace Greeley, abolitionist Frederick Douglass, Clarence Darrow, Christopher Morley, Lincoln Steffens, O.E. Rolvaag, Carl Sandburg, John Dewey, Carry Nation, Will Durant, Thomas Hart Benton and Archibald MacLeish.

The University Lecture Series brought some of the speakers to town; others were sponsored by the Saturday Luncheon Club or by the Times Club.

1958

Burge Hall dormitory built, named for Adelaide Burge, dean of women, 1922-42; senior counselor, 1942-45.

First U.S. earth satellite, Explorer I, carries cosmic ray instruments built at the UI.

Computer Center established, renamed Weeg Computing Center in 1978 for Gerard P. Weeg, director, 1964-77.

1959

American College Testing Program, developed by UI testing program, established.

1960

Size of campus tripled and University staff doubled since 1940.

Hawkeye Drive Apartments (married student housing) built.

1961

Enrollment 11,701.

Institute of Public Affairs moves into historic Dey House, 507 North Clinton Street (built in 1857, acquired by UI in 1948).

1962

Addition to Law Center built.

1963

Pharmacy Building constructed.

1964

University Hospital South Wing built.

Daum Hall dormitory built, named for Dr. Kate Daum, professor of dietetics and director of nutrition at University Hospitals, 1943-55; joined faculty in 1926.

Department of Art becomes School of Art and Art History.

Enrollment 14,480.

1965

Oakdale Hospital, built in 1914, designated for use of Board of Regents by state.

Nation's first Pharmacology-Toxicology Center established at Oakdale.

Phillips Hall (College of Business Administration) built, named for Chester A. Phillips, dean of the College of Business Administration, 1920-52, and UI acting president, 1940.

Physics Research Center built, renamed Van Allen Hall for James Van Allen, head of the Physics and Astronomy Department since 1951.

Enrollment 16,355.

The Black Angel

Until you were kissed in front of the Black Angel, you weren't a true coed, according to an early UI tradition. The Black Angel, a monument to the Feldevert family in Oakland Cemetery, was cast in bronze in 1912 and turned black from oxidation. A whole raft of legends and superstitions surrounds the unusual sculpture.

Buried at Oakland are Robert Lucas, first governor of the Territory of Iowa, 1838-41, and Samuel J. Kirkwood, Iowa's Civil War governor, 1860-64, three UI presidents—Charles A. Schaeffer, Walter A. Jessup and Virgil M. Hancher—and an acting president, Chester A. Phillips.

Each May, the College of Medicine conducts a memorial service at Oakland for those who willed their bodies to research at the University of Iowa Hospitals and Clinics.

Stone ornamentation on Schaeffer Hall.

1965-71

Period of great unrest and violence on campus. Protests center on Vietnam War, Kent State killings, invasion of Cambodia and recruiting on campus by U.S. Marines and chemical companies. Sit-in at Office of Student Affairs. Downtown windows smashed by demonstrators. Rhetoric Building (Old Armory-temporary) burned. Old Capitol broken into and smoke-bombed. Tear gas used by police.

1966

Center for New Music established.

Stanley Hall dormitory built, named for Carrie Stanley, a professor in the Department of English, 1920-52.

English-Philosophy Building constructed.

Rienow Hall dormitory built, named for Robert E. Rienow, dean of men, 1918-42; senior counselor, 1942-45.

Agricultural Medicine Research Facility built on Oakdale campus.

1967

International Writing Program started by Prof. Paul Engle.

Jefferson Building acquired (built as hotel in 1913).

School of Library Science established.

1968

Rienow II dormitory built, renamed Slater Hall for Fred "Duke" Slater, all-America tackle on the 1921 championship football team.

Wendell Johnson Speech and Hearing Center erected. Dr. Johnson was on the faculty of the Department of Speech Pathology, 1937-65; director of Speech Clinic, 1945-65.

Graphic Services Building occupied.

Hawkeye Court Apartments (married student housing) built.

1969

Afro-American Studies, an interdisciplinary program, established.

Museum of Art opened, financed by private donations.

Spence Laboratories of Psychology built, named for Dr. Kenneth Spence, head of the Department of Psychology, 1942-64.

Addition to Iowa Memorial Union built. Enrollment 20,236.

1970

Recreation Building constructed.

1971

Music Building and Nursing Building erected.

What Next?

Student shenanigans of one sort or another have disturbed the peace in Iowa City periodically through the years. Most of them have been harmless, such as the "panty raids" of the 1950s when a gang of male students would gather at a women's dorm or sorority and with great hilarity beseech the occupants to toss their underthings out the windows. Later, there were bra-burnings to dramatize women's liberation. And in the mid-1970s "streaking" was the fad. More than one nude body flashed across the Pentacrest grounds and across Dubuque Street in the Fraternity Row area.

A brass replica of the original key to Old Capitol is one of the souvenirs available at Old Capitol Gift Shop.

Turbulent Times

Violent demonstrations rocked campuses in the late 1960s and early 1970s. Student anger at the Vietnam War caused many colleges and universities to close, but President Willard L. Boyd kept the UI open. However, the situation became so tense that in the spring of 1970, students were given the option of leaving the campus before finals. They could accept their current grades, take incompletes in all courses or accept P (pass) or W (withdraw) in each course. The fourth option was to stay in school. About 12,000 students, nearly two-thirds of the total enrollment, chose to leave the campus.

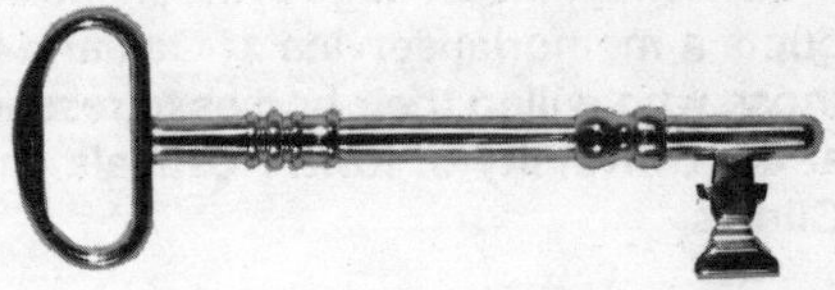

Industrialist Roy J. Carver of Muscatine, Iowa, gives $3.5 million in stock to the University (later sold for $4.2 million). Funds used for UI College of Medicine model community health center in Muscatine, 10 scholarships to needy students, endowment of five distinguished professorships, an addition to Museum of Art, restoration of Old Capitol's House Chamber, furnishing of Hancher Auditorium, artificial turf for Kinnick Stadium and support of President's Academic Development Fund.

1972

Hancher Auditorium opens, named for Virgil M. Hancher, UI president, 1940-64.

Opening of Clapp Recital Hall, named for Philip Greeley Clapp, head of the Department of Music, 1919-54, and Harper Hall, named for Earl E. Harper, director of School of Fine Arts and of Iowa Memorial Union, 1938-63, in Music Building.

Beer and wine allowed in Union and in dormitories.

1972-76

Old Capitol restored, placed on National Register of Historic Places in 1972 and named a National Historic Landmark in 1976.

1973

Bowen Science Building (Basic Sciences) built, named for Howard R. Bowen, UI president, 1964-69.

Lindquist Center built, named for E.F. Lindquist, professor in the Department of Education, 1925-57; director of Iowa Testing Program, 1957-72.

Dental Science Building and Main Library addition constructed.

1974

Health Sciences Library erected.

Roy J. Carver gives additional $3.7 million to help build addition to University Hospitals and Clinics (including heliport pad), $1.5 million for a Professorship of Internal Medicine and $200,000 to support a program to develop UI Health Center.

1975

Last of the "temporary" barracks used for married housing after World War II come tumbling down. Earlier, barracks removed to make way for Hospital School, Dental Science Building, the proposed Hancher Auditorium and stadium parking.

It's a Mystery

It was Dec. 18, 1970, and the restorers of Old Capitol watched eagerly as the southeast cornerstone dated 1840 was removed. Everyone assumed it held a copper box containing the original plans for the building. Surprise! No copper box. No place for such a box. Also, no plans to search further for the elusive receptacle.

Whetstone's

For over a century—1868 until the early 1970s—Whetstone's Drug Store at the corner of Clinton and Washington streets was a favorite hangout for students to meet for soft drinks and chatter and to mail home their laundry boxes at the postal substation. More than a student hangout, it was a landmark, a campus institution. A standard goodbye was "Meet you at Whet's."

The Governor's office in Old Capitol with its fireplace, wood box, rocking chair and walnut secretary reflect a homey atmosphere. The carpeting is ingrain. After the government moved to Des Moines, the room was used for classrooms.

1976

Carver Wing at Museum of Art constructed.

Seven-story North Tower addition opens at University Hospitals, renamed Boyd Tower in 1981 for Willard L. Boyd, UI president, 1969-81, and his wife, Susan.

Alumni Center built adjoining Museum of Art.

1977

Hawkeye Park Apartments (married student housing) built.

1978

Roy J. Carver Pavilion Phase A opens at University Hospitals and Clinics.

1979

College of Education moves into second section of Lindquist Center.

1980

Enrollment 25,100.

1982

Colloton Pavilion Phase A opens at University Hospitals, named for John Colloton, director of University Hospitals and Clinics since 1972 and assistant to the president for statewide health services since 1978.

Enrollment 28,140.

1983

Carver-Hawkeye Arena opens for basketball, wrestling and other activities. Roy J. Carver gives more than $1 million of the $10 million contributed to the Hawkeye Arena/Recreation Campaign. Outdoor playing fields expanded and Field House remodeled.

Mayflower Apartments acquired for residence hall. (Built in 1966.)

Enrollment 29,600.

UI primarily a liberal arts university with 60 percent of its students enrolled in that college.

But Not Forgotten

Restaurants now on Memory Lane include the D and L, the Capitol, Reich's, Smith's, the Princess, and two tearooms (Town and Gown—above what is now Seiferts—and the Mad Hatter's). There no longer is a Huddle in the Jefferson Hotel, nor for that matter, the hotel either. Now called the Jefferson Building, it belongs to the University and houses various University services. Also a part of bygone days were Racine's Cigar Stores and two student favorites on Iowa Avenue—the Hamburg Inn and Sidwell's (for ice cream cones).

Trademarks

In the murky past, you could tell a law student because of his cane, a dental student because of his derby hat and a freshman because of his green beanie.

Right Here in River City

Canoeing on the Iowa River is one of the more sprightly campus activities with sometimes as many as 100 canoes at one time plying the placid river.

The Fitzgerald Boathouse, which was just north of the Union, was a campus fixture from 1906 until it was torn down in the 1950s. The University now rents the canoes, and the boathouse is across the river and upstream from where the old boathouse was located.

Rhetoric is a Must

Rhetoric (a course combining reading, writing and speech) is the only course required of all undergraduates at the UI today.

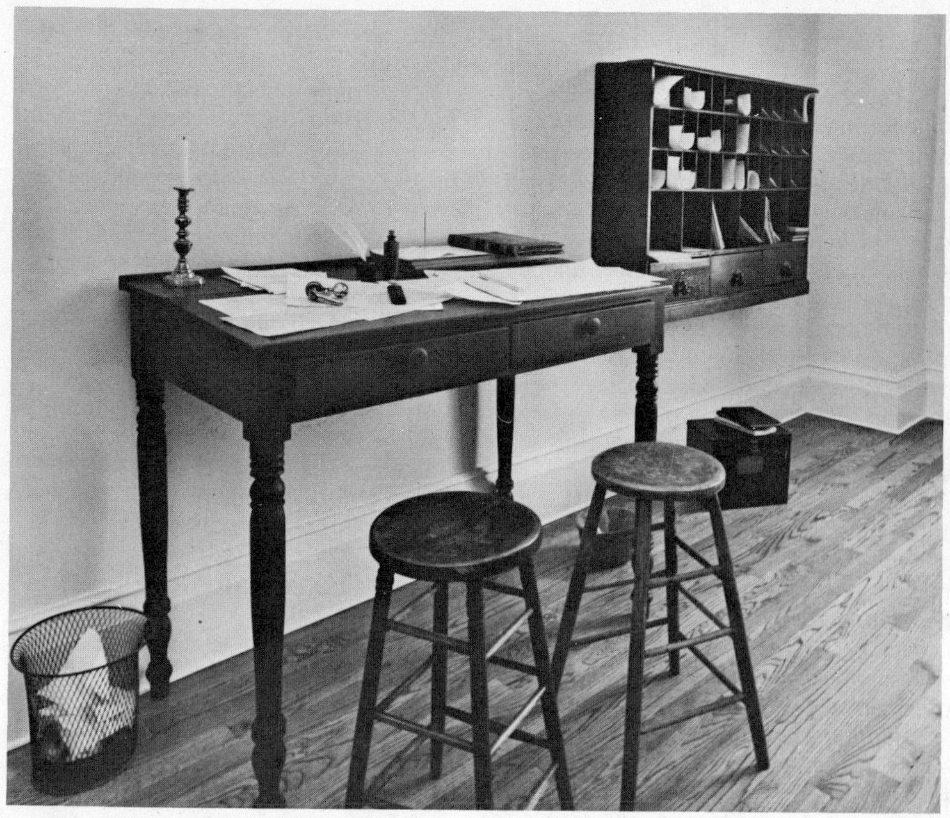

The Auditor's Office, Old Capitol.

Flexible

The UI is flexible. Courses are offered at night, on Saturdays, by mail, on radio and television, in newspapers, in extension courses in various cities and by the telebridge phone system. Through CLEP (College-Level Examination Program), you can test out of certain courses.

Indeed, you can get a degree from the UI without ever setting foot in Iowa City. It's a Bachelor of Liberal Studies degree. The program is administered by the Division of Continuing Education and is open to those who have Associate in Arts degrees.

Riding High

Cambus, the University bus system on which students, faculty, townspeople and visitors all ride free, has a whopping annual ridership of 2½ million.

Departments

Editor's Note: If something herein is called a department that is now a school, don't fret. Within a university, departments have a way of becoming schools, which in turn have a way of becoming colleges. We have tried to refer with historical accuracy to these divisions at particular points in time.

Morally Speaking

Today the University feels less responsible for the morals of "the daughters and sons of Old Gold" than it did in the past.

Attendance at morning chapel was mandatory until 1882. Men and women students were not allowed to converse with each other 15 minutes before chapel.

Students were expected to go to church on Sundays. Roll was called each morning at 7:45 before chapel. On Monday mornings each student had to say if he or she had gone to church the day before. (For some reason, law students were exempt.)

Campus regulations in the 1870s were strict and precise: "Every student shall attend punctually at morning prayers . . . recitations and lectures . . . when absent, he shall tender an excuse in writing.

"Students . . . are not . . . to leave the city without the knowledge and consent of the president . . .

"Students are prohibited from visiting saloons, tippling houses, gaming houses, billiard rooms, and theaters; from using obscene or profane language; from playing cards or any game of chance for money or any kind of wager.

"No student shall use intoxicating drinks, or keep them in his room or possession, or offer them to others to drink; and any student (found) guilty of being intoxicated shall be promptly dismissed from the university.

"For every breach of good morals or good order, a reduction will be made from the standing of the student . . .

"Ladies are not to wear their bonnets during recitations."

Rules for student conduct gradually became more and more lenient in line with the tempo of the times. No longer are freshmen required to live in a residence hall.

Curfew for women was firmly established until recent years. Women's hours were 10 p.m. weeknights and midnight on weekends, until 1937. However, University plays often were not over by 10 and women students had to leave before the final curtain. A half-hour was added, and 10:30 weeknights, 12:30 weekends was the rule.

The penalty for being late was firmly enforced: confinement in the dormitory the next weekend. Those minutes late added up. The culprit gave up a weekend for each 10 minutes of lateness.

The bewitching hour was pushed forward in 1961. Hours became 11 p.m. Sunday through Thursday for freshmen women and midnight for sophomore women and 1 a.m. Friday and Saturday nights for both.

By 1963 each dormitory and sorority had the right to set its own hours.

Dormitories became coed in 1970-71. Today only one residence hall, Stanley, is reserved for women only.

Riverbanking

Different eras called it petting, pitching woo, necking, smooching or making out. In Iowa City, there's a specialized version called "riverbanking." It has probably been indulged in as long as there has been an Iowa River (and students).

Chug-a-lug

T.G.I.F. (Thank God It's Friday) continues as a campus celebration on the eve of the weekend, usually observed with beer and popcorn following Friday classes. Past generations will remember Joe's Place (which advertises as "the oldest student bar in town") and the Airliner (or 'Liner), which has been a campus hangout since 1944. Don's and Donnelly's exist only in memories.

How 'bout Them Hawks?

Bumper stickers proclaim, "It's great to be a Hawkeye." Thousands of Iowa fans agree as they flock to football and basketball games and to wrestling meets. The stands are a sea of gold and black shirts, caps and sweaters. Hawkeye fever is catching.

All three teams draw national attention and bring pride to Iowans. Coach Hayden Fry's football teams are bowl-minded. The 1981 team went to the Rose Bowl and the 1982 team to the Peach Bowl. Under Lute Olson, UI's basketball teams earned NCAA berths five years in a row (1979-83), a Big Ten record. The 1980 team finished fourth in the nation and set a school record of 23 wins. Olson was named 1980 national Coach of the Year. His teams won 167 games, a UI record. George Raveling is the current basketball coach. Coach Dan Gable, himself an Olympic wrestling champion, has led his teams to an unprecedented six NCAA championships, 1978 through 1983. He was the first man ever to win 100 matches as both a wrestler and a coach.

Men's Athletic Director Chalmers "Bump" Elliott oversees men's intercollegiate sports.

Golden eras of Iowa football include Alden Knipe's 1899 and 1900 teams (9 wins, 1 tie each year); Howard Jones' 1921 and 1922 teams (both undefeated); Dr. Eddie Anderson's Ironmen of 1939 (6-1-1) and Forest Evashevski's 1952-60 teams (two Big Ten championships, two wins in the Rose Bowl and the national championship in 1958).

Iowa has won four Big Ten basketball championships (1945, 1955, 1956 and 1970) and tied for four (1923, 1926, 1968 and 1979). Bucky O'Connor coached the 1955 Hawks to the NCAA semifinals, finishing fourth, and the "Fabulous Five" to the NCAA finals in 1956, finishing second to San Francisco. Ralph Miller's "Six Pack" had a 14-0 Big Ten record in 1970. The team scored 100 or more points in 14 games and *averaged* 98.7 points a game.

In the 1970s, women's intercollegiate athletics had an upsurge in interest, support, financing and scholarships. Federal guidelines in Title IX gave this area a big push. Under the direction of Dr. Christine Grant, women's athletic director, Iowa fields women's teams in 10 sports—basketball, volleyball, swimming, tennis, golf, gymnastics, field hockey, track and field, softball and cross-country.

Football Coaches

Hayden Fry 1979-present
Bob Commings 1974-78
Frank Lauterbur 1971-73
Ray Nagel 1966-70
Jerry Burns 1961-65
Forest Evashevski 1952-60
Len Raffensperger 1950-51
Clem Crowe 1945
E.P. Madigan 1943-44
Eddie Anderson 1939-42; 1946-49
Irl Tubbs 1937-38
O.M. Solem 1932-36
Burton Ingwersen 1924-31
Howard Jones 1916-23

Basketball Coaches

George Raveling 1983-present
Lute Olson 1975-83
Dick Schultz 1971-74
Ralph Miller 1965-70
Sharm Scheuerman 1959-64
Frank "Bucky" O'Connor 1952-58
Pops Harrison 1944-50
Rollie Williams 1930-43 and 1951

Whole Hog

A live pig was the bet between Gov. Clyde Herring of Iowa and Gov. Floyd Olson of Minnesota on the 1935 Iowa-Minnesota football game. Iowa lost, so Herring gave "Floyd of Rosedale," a champion porker, to Olson. Olson had a bronze sculpture made of his prize. Ever since, Floyd spends the year with the school winning the annual game.

Carver-Hawkeye Arena
Photos above and on page 47

In the huge Carver-Hawkeye Arena, spectators sit in comfortable theater-type seats with molded backs, their views of the floor unobstructed, a far cry from the old Field House a half-mile away. Opened in 1983, the 15,283-seat arena hunkers down partly below ground in a wooded ravine on the west campus. Its 3½-acre roof with exposed steel trusses adds a dramatic touch to the unusual design. Entrance is at ground level, and spectators walk down one of 28 aisles to their seats. On the ground level concourse, a quarter of a mile around, are eight concession stands, including the Hawk Shop.

The arena is used for wrestling, men's and women's basketball, volleyball, gymnastics, tennis, concerts and other University functions. Attached to the arena is a 60,000-square foot Athletic Office Building holding offices of athletic directors and staff, the main ticket office and the sports information office. On the third level are three rooms honoring individuals. They are the George C. Foerstner Iowa Room, the Robert F. Ray Big Ten Room and the Men's Basketball Coaches' Conference Room, honoring B.L. "Bill" Baines, arena construction director.

Foerstner, founder and retired chairman of Amana Refrigeration Inc., a subsidiary of Raytheon Company, is one of UI's biggest athletic boosters. His company sponsors the Amana VIP Golf Tournament, which annually brings profes-sional golfers and Amana Refrigeration dealers to UI's Finkbine golf course for a one-day meet. Proceeds go into a fund to support men's and women's athletic programs at UI.

The late Dean Ray was the Big Ten faculty representative for The University of Iowa for 26 years.

Kinnick Stadium
Photos on pages 44-45 and 46

"I thank God that I was born to the gridirons of the Middle West and not to the battlefields of Europe. I can speak confidently that the football players of this country would much rather fight for the Heisman Trophy than for the Croix de Guerre."

> —*Nile Kinnick, winner of the Heisman award in 1939, in his acceptance speech.*

Kinnick Stadium explodes with excitement every football Saturday when loyal Iowa fans cheer their beloved Hawks. Built in 1929, enlarged in 1983, the stadium seats 65,000. It was renamed in 1972 to honor Nile Kinnick, famed halfback on the legendary Ironmen football team of 1939. Kinnick was a consensus all-America, UI's only Heisman Trophy winner ("the best college football player in the country") and a Phi Beta Kappa. A Navy pilot in World War II, he was killed June 2, 1943, in a forced landing over the Caribbean Sea. His jersey number 24 has been retired. Kinnick's likeness is on the heads side of the official Big Ten game coin.

Herky the Hawk

Photo on page 47

Good ol' stiff-arming Herky the Hawk, Iowa's official athletic mascot, has gone through several mutations since his hatching in 1948. A journalism instructor, Richard Spencer III, fathered the feathered symbol after studying stuffed birds at the Museum of Natural History.

When football coach Hayden Fry arrived in 1978, he gave Herky a face lift, and the ferocious "Tiger Hawk" emerged.

"Live" Herkys stir up spirit at athletic events. A generic, all-purpose Herky in an "I" sweater but not dressed in the uniform of a specific sport now represents all sports, including women's—except football, where the Tiger Hawk still flies. Since 1961, Delta Tau Delta fraternity members have taken turns "being Herky."

Herky went to war during the Korean conflict as the insignia of the 124th fighter squadron. The Tiger Hawk flew on the space shuttle *Columbia* in March 1982, painted on the plasma diagnostic package designed and built at The University of Iowa.

Sing-along

Pep songs drum up that old college spirit at Hawkeye athletic events, and "The Old Gold Hymn" evokes feelings of loyalty and nostalgia.

"On Iowa," written by W.R. Law, class of 1904, has been popular ever since its introduction at a 1919 pep rally on the eve of the Iowa-South Dakota football game.

Of more recent vintage, the "Iowa Fight Song" was written by Meredith Willson, native of Mason City, Iowa, and composer of *The Music Man*. It was first heard nationwide Dec. 31, 1950, on "The Big Show," the NBC radio program starring Willson and Talullah Bankhead. It was introduced to the University at the Iowa-Indiana basketball game Feb. 12, 1951.

"The Old Gold Hymn" is sung to the tune of "Believe Me, If All Those Endearing Young Charms" with words written by John C. Parrish. In 1905, it won the prize offered by President George E. MacLean in a song contest.

Homecoming Hoopla

Homecomings of yore meant corn monuments on the Pentacrest, pep rallies with bonfires and cheerleaders, parades with floats and marching bands, badges, a dance, a queen.

Corn monuments and bonfires are no longer in vogue, but the other traditions, some dating to the first Homecoming in 1912, still prevail.

Interest flagged in the late 1960s and 1970s. In 1972, it wasn't even called Homecoming; it was Old Capitol Week. The Homecoming Dance was dropped in 1971, not to be revived until 10 years later.

Today, there is a resurgence of enthusiasm for the venerable event. A modern-day tradition was born in 1973 when the Alumni Marching Band, wearing gold vests and gold "I" caps, made its debut at halftime of the Homecoming game.

One of the most enduring, and endearing, traditions is the Homecoming badge. Earliest badges pictured the team, the coach flanked by the captains, with team members clustered around.

It wasn't until 1931 that a hawk was pictured, but after Herky's conception by Richard Spencer in 1948, the bird appeared in many guises and situations—dressed as a Scottish Highlander in 1954 and riding on a rocket in 1958 in honor of Dr. James Van Allen's space exploration.

During World War II, the 1942 badge showed a hawk carrying a "V" for victory. Buyers were asked to return the badges so they could be used for scrap in the war effort. In 1943, a cardboard tag replaced the usual metal badge.

The 1969 badge pictured a Michigan State Spartan speared with a nail. The student committee chose "Screw 'em, Hawks!" for the motto. When the badges were delivered, the words had been changed to "Nail 'em, Hawks!"

The DI

The *University Reporter*, granddaddy of the *Daily Iowan*, first appeared in 1868. It merged with the *Vidette* (1879-81) to form the *Vidette-Reporter* in 1881, which together with the *SUI Quill* begat the *Daily Iowan* in 1901. The *DI* is published daily except Sunday and prints 19,000 copies, delivering to the residences of University students. The *Daily Iowan* is managed by the Board of Student Publications, Inc., and is a member of the Associated Press. In 1975, the Iowa Press Association named it "Newspaper of the Year."

Haw-Haw-Hawkeye

The first humor magazine on campus was called *Haw-Haw-Hawkeye*. It had a short life, only one issue, June, 1910. One of its successors, *Frivol*, fared much better, lasting 32 years, from 1919 to 1951.

The Hawkeye's Back

The *Hawkeye* yearbook is back. From 1973 to 1977, no *Hawkeye* was printed. First published in 1892, the book was sponsored traditionally by the junior class. In 1945, a change was made to a senior book, so it fell to the Class of '46 to sponsor the *Hawkeye* both as juniors and seniors. At least they had their "mug shots" in twice!

'Rhythm Rambles'

"It's 12 o'clock and 'Stardust' means *Rhythm Rambles!*" For 46 years that cheery greeting and the strains of Hoagy Carmichael's tune were heard at noon on radio station WSUI. The 30 minutes of popular music that followed brought gladness to the hearts, ears and dancing feet of two generations of Iowa youth.

Rhythm Rambles, 1935-81, was considered the longest-running program on any educational radio station in America. The program was dropped when WSUI became more news and information oriented and the musical emphasis moved to the University's FM station, KSUI.

A Bonnie Group

The skirl of bagpipes and the measured beat of drums announced the arrival of the Scottish Highlander Band at Iowa football games for 45 years. No other Big Ten school had a bagpipe band, and the group was identified with the UI wherever it went.

Colorful uniforms consisted of red, green and navy plaid kilts (Stewart tartan), woolen jackets, and white spats and gloves.

Col. George Dailey of the Department of Military Science organized the unit in 1935, and Bill Adamson was director from 1937 until his death in 1965.

In its heyday, the group played all over the United States and took European tours every four years.

At first all-male, the band switched to all-female during World War II and didn't accept males again until 1972. Interest flagged and Highlanders is now a small coed student organization.

Mountain Climbers

Without a mountain in sight, the Iowa Mountaineers is the largest university mountaineering organization in the world with a membership of 500-650 from all over the U.S.

Since John Ebert, retired chief radio and sound engineer for the University, and his wife, Ede, founded the club in 1940, it has guided more than 14,000 people in alpine climbing in 15 countries on six continents.

"The University is the instrument that will provide the best multiplier, over many years, for the things that will benefit the people..."

—*Philanthropist Roy J. Carver*

A 1924 photograph taken from Newton Road shows the Iowa Avenue Bridge, Iowa Field, the Pentacrest and, at left, Women's Gymnasium (Halsey), Calvin Hall, College of Law Building (Gilmore) and Old Dental Building.

All for Iowa

Alumni strengthen UI with their loyalty as well as their financial help. The Iowa Alumni Association was organized in 1867. In 1947, Loren Hickerson became the first full-time executive secretary.

The Old Capitol Club, organized in 1974, is the highest level of membership in the association.

The Old Gold Development Fund in 1955 began encouraging annual alumni giving. It was the forerunner of The University of Iowa Foundation, which was organized in 1956 to seek and receive private gifts and bequests for the University.

The University's most generous benefactors (alumni and non-alumni) are recognized by the UI Foundation through membership in The Presidents Club of The University of Iowa.

Pulitzer Winners

Alumni who have won Pulitzer Prizes include Marquis W. Childs, James A. McPherson, Donald Justice, Tracy Kidder, Wallace E. Stegner, Paul F. Conrad (two) and Tennessee Williams (two).

Arctic Explorer

Vilhjalmur Stefansson (1879-1962), Arctic explorer and writer, was a 1903 graduate of UI. On his second expedition (1908-12), he discovered "blond" Eskimos who had never seen a white man. A Stefansson bust by Emanuel Otto Haln of Canada is permanently on display in the foyer of Macbride Hall. Stefansson wrote 24 books and 400 articles about the far north.

Photo by Kent

When Fred Kent was a student, his pictures of athletic games became postcards which sold at Whetstone's Drug Store for a nickel each. After his graduation in 1915, he became the University's official photographer, and he headed the UI's Photographic Service for many years. Named for him is the 200-acre F.W. Kent Park on Highway 6 west of Iowa City. In its timber he found many of the owls he photographed.

The Gallup Poll

George Gallup, called "the father of modern public opinion polls," received B.A., M.A. and Ph.D. degrees from the UI. He was editor of the *Daily Iowan* and taught journalism and psychology at the University from 1923 to 1929. Since 1935, he has been reporting public opinion once a week. He was the *Time* magazine cover story May 3, 1948. Scandinavians have no word for survey or poll, so they refer to "a gallup," generically.

Dropped One 'l'

Famed puppeteer Bil Baird, who has been putting on puppet shows on Broadway, in films and on TV for over 50 years, was head cheerleader when he attended the UI. He put on puppet shows during intermission of University band concerts. After graduating in 1926, he dropped an "l" from his first name. He says nobody ever pronounced that second "l" anyway!

The Hot Line

Jess Gorkin, a 1936 graduate of the UI and editor of the *Daily Iowan*, came up with an idea whose time had come. While an editor of *Parade* magazine, he conceived of a hot line (a direct Teletype circuit) between Washington and Moscow to prevent accidental nuclear war. He contacted the President and the Premier, pursued the idea and it became a reality in 1963.

Champion

George Nissen, a 1937 graduate, invented a foldable, portable trampoline for acrobatic tumbling and mass-produces it in his Cedar Rapids factory. The Nissen Corporation, a division of Kidde, Inc., ships trampolines and other gymnastic equipment all over the world. Nissen was a national tumbling champion in 1935, 1936 and 1937 and an all-America diver in 1937.

We Called Him 'Tennessee'

Thomas Lanier Williams was just plain "Tom" when he came to the UI as a senior in 1937, but his classmates quickly nicknamed him "Tennessee" because of his Southern accent. He liked it and used it on a short story published after his graduation in 1938.

Actually, he wasn't even from Tennessee, although his ancestors were. His family lived in St. Louis.

He wrote a series of highly successful plays, including two Pulitzer Prize winners, *A Streetcar Named Desire* in 1948 and *Cat on a Hot Tin Roof* in 1955. He also penned *The Glass Menagerie*, *The Rose Tattoo*, *Suddenly Last Summer* and *Sweet Bird of Youth*, among others.

He failed his second semester at Iowa and needed a summer session to graduate. In his *Tennessee Williams: Memoirs* (Doubleday and Co., Inc.), he writes: "That single summer at Iowa, I was still lonely, and I took to wandering about the streets at night to escape the stifling heat of my room. There were many great trees and the town had an old-fashioned charm. At night it almost seemed Southern . . . ."

Contrary to popular supposition, he was not in the Writers' Workshop. He was a student in the drama department.

Honored Guard

A guard on the famous 1939 Ironmen football team, Max S. Hawkins, has a street named in his honor. Hawkins Drive is a four-lane roadway connecting Highways 6 and 218 with Woolf Avenue, providing access to the arena and the stadium. Hawkins was the UI's director of state relations from 1970 to 1981. Before that, he was field secretary for the Alumni Association.

Back to Bach

One of the most popular classes in the 1940s was "Little Known Religious Groups in America," taught by Dr. Marcus Bach of the School of Religion, and aired on the campus radio station, WSUI. Dr. Bach lectured widely on the subjects of interfaith understanding and the contemporary religious scene. He wrote many books and plays, including *They Have Found a Faith* and *Report to Protestants*.

This Way Up

Astronaut and U.S. Senator John Glenn attended the UI's Navy pre-flight school in 1942. Twenty years later, he became the first American in orbit, circling the earth three times in a Mercury space capsule.

Claims to Fame

Paul F. Conrad, a 1950 graduate, is a political cartoonist for the *Los Angeles Times*, the winner of two Pulitzer Prizes and the subject of a *Time* magazine cover story. Other claims to fame: Before coming to UI, he flunked out of Iowa State where he was studying architecture. And he made the Nixon enemy list.

Those in Flicks

Show biz greats who were once UI students include actors MacDonald Carey; Greg Morris ("Mission: Impossible"), who went to UI to play basketball but got turned on by drama; Alex Karras (also a UI all-America football player in the 1950s); Gene Wilder and Mary Beth Hurt; TV producer and director Norman Felton; Charles Guggenheim, winner of two Academy Awards for producing documentary films; and Duck's Breath Mystery Theater, a comedy group founded in Iowa City in 1975, transported to San Francisco and heard over National Public Radio.

Nick (Nicholas) Meyer, award-winning film writer/director/best-selling novelist, is the author of *The Seven Percent Solution*. His film, *Time After Time*, was given its U.S. premier at Hancher Auditorium.

She Chose Stardom

Jean Seberg of Marshalltown, Iowa, was an almost-freshman at UI in 1956 when her future took a dramatic turn. She promised her father she would enroll at the University if he would drive her to Chicago to audition for the part of Joan of Arc in the film *St. Joan*. Jean went to Iowa City, met her roommate and pledged her sister's sorority, Kappa Alpha Theta. She read for director Otto Preminger Sept. 15. The rest, as they say, is history. After a stormy career, she died in Paris in 1979.

'What's Opera?'

The grandson of a slave, the son of a coalminer, Simon Estes of Centerville, Iowa, dreamed of being a doctor. A pre-med student at the UI in the late 1950s, he did menial jobs to support himself. He switched to theology and psychology and decided to try out for the UI chorus. He failed the tryout, but he took the director's advice and tried out for the Old Gold Singers, a 22-voice song-and-dance troupe performing popular music. He became the first black member and a soloist. When Prof. Charles Kellis, a voice instructor, heard him sing, he said, "You could sing opera." "What's opera?" Estes asked. At the urging of Prof. Kellis, Estes auditioned at the Juilliard School of Music and received a full scholarship. He proceeded to win a medal at the 1966 Tchaikovsky competition in Moscow, to sing in the great opera houses of Europe and to become a bass-baritone on the roster of the Metropolitan Opera Company of New York City. And yes, he can now define "opera."

Lindquist Center

Photo on page 40

The Lindquist Center is one of the most interesting buildings on the east campus. Five- and six-sided rooms are brightly decorated with Scandinavian art. In the courtyard is a graceful sculpture by Louise Nevelson. The center was named in honor of the late E.F. Lindquist, founder of Iowa's testing programs. Considered the father of modern educational testing, he invented the first electronic test scoring machine. His work at the UI brought about the Iowa Tests of Basic Skills and the Iowa Tests of Educational Development. The American College Testing Program and the Westinghouse Learning Corporation's Measurement Research Center, outgrowths of the University's research, have made Iowa City a world center for educational testing.

Dean of Deans

Thanks to the pioneering efforts of Carl E. Seashore, the interdisciplinary science of speech pathology was born at the UI in 1897. Head of the Department of Psychology from 1905 to 1942, Dr. Seashore researched child and abnormal psychology and the psychology of music. He devised the Seashore Measures of Musical Talent to test for musical aptitude. As head of the Graduate School (1908-36 and 1942-46) he is credited with promoting the revolutionary idea of accepting creative work for advanced degrees in lieu of theses.

Ladd and the Law

Mason Ladd, who joined the faculty in 1929 and was dean of the UI College of Law from 1939 to 1966, was a nationally known authority on the law of evidence. He wrote three law books and co-authored three others. After retiring from UI in 1966, he became the first dean of the law school at Florida State University (1966-69) and had the unusual distinction of holding the title of dean emeritus from both schools. The UI law school has a Mason Ladd Distinguished Professorship.

In Love with UI

Benjamin F. Shambaugh so loved the University that he had his ashes scattered over the western slopes of the Old Capitol grounds.

Head of the Political Science Department from 1900 to 1940, he was one of Iowa's most beloved professors. From 1907 to 1940 he headed the State Historical Society of Iowa, which published his book, *The Old Stone Capitol Remembers*. He was so clever at introducing the speaker at the University Lecture Series that sometimes the introduction was better than the speech.

Shambaugh Auditorium in the Main Library, Shambaugh House and the Shambaugh Lectureship are all named for him.

Bertha Shambaugh was noted for her histories of the Amana Colonies, the Community of True Inspiration.

Prof. and Mrs. Shambaugh frequently entertained students, professors and visiting lecturers at dinner. Leaving nothing to chance, they would place a list of conversational topics beside each plate.

The Shambaughs gave their home at 219 North Clinton Street to the University. Built in 1902, it was first used by the UI as a guest house for visiting dignitaries and is now the Honors Center of the University.

Speech Problems

Wendell Johnson, a UI faculty member for 35 years, was nationally recognized for his work with stutterers. He knew whereof he spoke, having a severe stuttering problem himself. While a student at UI he had been one of the subjects of a research program on speech defects. In his clinical work he was credited with personally helping some 2500 stutterers. The Wendell Johnson Speech and Hearing Center, built in 1968, contains the Department of Speech Pathology and Audiology and the Speech and Hearing Clinic. Dr. Johnson was on the faculty from 1937 to 1965 and director of the clinic from 1945 to 1965.

James Van Allen

If having your likeness on the cover of *Time* magazine symbolizes success, UI's James Van Allen gets two gold stars. He had the cover to himself May 4, 1959, and shared it with 14 other scientists as "Men of the Year" Jan. 2, 1961. In the 1959 article, *Time* called the lab in the basement of the UI Physics Building, now MacLean Hall, "the most famed space-instrument laboratory in the U.S." and Dr. Van Allen "the U.S.'s foremost space scientist."

An authority on man-made satellites and instrumentation of rockets, Dr. Van Allen became head of the Department of Physics and Astronomy in 1951. He and his students designed and built the radiation detection instruments on Explorer I, the first successful American satellite. More than 40 spacecrafts have carried UI instruments. UI is the only university in the world where space research satellites have been completely designed and built.

When he discovered the concentration of particles of energy in the Earth's outer magnetic field in 1958, they were named the Van Allen radiation belts in his honor. With his discovery, a new field of study was born—magnetospheric physics.

In 1979, Dr. Van Allen discovered Saturn's twelfth moon, and he broke the news, not at a press conference, but to students in his introductory astronomy class. He takes his fame lightly and continues to teach an undergraduate class each year.

Dr. Van Allen is continuing to analyze and interpret cosmic ray data from his instruments on Pioneers 10 and 11 in the outer solar system, including a search for the heliopause, the outer boundary of the flow of the solar wind. He is also analyzing magnetic field data from the Hawkeye satellite (designed and built at the UI) in the outer reaches of the earth's magnetosphere. Another project is the Galileo project, in which a spacecraft will become the first artificial satellite of the remote planet, Jupiter.

Dr. Van Allen's book, *Origins of Magnetospheric Physics*, was published by the Smithsonian Institution in 1983.

Iowa Memorial Union
Photo on page 48

Iowa Memorial Union is a campus center for extracurricular activities. Built in 1926 as a memorial to students who died in World War I, it was expanded in 1955. Adjoining the Union is Iowa House, a hotel for visitors on campus. The Union houses food services, bowling and billiards, a barber shop, bookstore, television room, lounges and a movie theatre in addition to various student services.

Danforth Chapel
Photo on page 51

Tiny Danforth Chapel with its white spire sits on the east bank of the Iowa River next to Iowa Memorial Union. Built in 1952, it is a replica of an 1874 Iowa country church. It is nonsectarian, nondenominational and open to anyone in the University community for weddings, baptisms, meetings or meditation. Seating is limited to 75.

Furnishings are simple wooden benches, altar and cross. The Hammond organ was a gift of the Class of 1952.

The original church was discovered by Dr. R.F. Fitzgerald, then director of the School of Fine Arts. He showed it to Grant Wood, then an art professor at UI. They planned to move the church to the campus for a shrine to hold Wood's murals, but the building proved too fragile to move.

The red brick chapel was named for William H. Danforth, whose contribution (and that of the Danforth Foundation) helped fund its construction.

Danforth Chapel was open daily until 1967 when vandalism forced it to be closed except by appointment.

University Library
Photo on page 40

The Main Library is one of the largest buildings on campus. Occupying one square block, it is bounded by Washington, Madison and College streets. The five-story building contains over a million books and 20,000 periodical titles and can seat 4,000 students at tables. The University Library system is the largest in the state. The Main Library houses many special collections, such as the Leigh Hunt Collection of Hunt's letters, manuscripts and editions of his work; the Mark Ranney Memorial Collection of 3,700 deluxe editions; the French Revolution Collection of more than 8,000 political pamphlets and French publications of 1788-1799; the John Springer Collection on typography; the "Ding" Darling Collection of nearly 6,000 original political cartoons; the Bollinger-Lincoln Collection (one of the best libraries of Lincolniana in the country); the "X" Collection of rare books; the Manuscript Collection of more than 10,000 letters and manuscripts of authors or historical figures; the Presidential Letters (original letters from all U.S. presidents) and manuscripts and editions of works by Iowa authors.

In the Health Sciences Library is the John Martin Ràre Book Room, which houses 2,000 volumes on the history of medicine. Dr. Martin's gift of his collection is the nucleus.

Presidents' Gallery

Portraits of all 15 former presidents of UI hang in the Presidents' Gallery on the fifth floor of the Main Library. All are oils except for the enlarged photograph of John Bowman and the four charcoal sketches which artist Cloy Kent of Iowa City created from old photographs. Willard L. Boyd's portrait was painted by Joseph Patrick of the School of Art and Art History faculty and Howard R. Bowen's by James Lechay, now retired from the School of Art and Art History.

Mosaic seal in the floor of Iowa Hall in Macbride Hall.

Museum of Natural History
Photo on page 41

Iowa Hall, a 6,000-square-foot gallery showing geologic, environmental and cultural history of the state of Iowa, is part of the renovated (1984) UI Museum of Natural History in Macbride Hall.

Life-sized scenes and landscapes of Iowa reach back 12,000 years into history. One of the 56 exhibits is a nine-foot-tall Pleistocene sloth.

Bird Hall and Mammal Hall are mainstays of the museum. Their exhibits on the third floor of Macbride include many natural habitat settings.

Of special interest is the Laysan Island Cyclorama, which displays specimens collected during the UI's Laysan Island expedition of 1911.

Founded in 1858 by an act of the General Assembly, the museum is the oldest university museum west of the Mississippi. Macbride Hall was built in 1907 to house the collection, which includes more than a million indexed specimens.

Attracting more than 42,000 visitors a year, the museum is open from 8 a.m. to 5 p.m. Monday through Saturday and 12:30 to 4:30 p.m. Sunday. Tours are available.

The School of Music with Clapp Recital Hall and Hancher Auditorium rising behind it.

Arts at UI

Art with a capital "A" adds its special magic to the Iowa City scene. Music, drama, dance, literature and the visual arts abound for the appreciator as well as for the student.

A group of buildings hugging the west bank of the Iowa River forms the Iowa Center for the Arts. When Hancher Auditorium was added to the complex in 1972, there was much ado about something. It is a jewel of a performing arts facility, a bit of Broadway and Carnegie Hall, bringing topnotch entertainment to eastern Iowa. Merely walking into its spacious lobby is an aesthetic experience.

Hancher connects with the Music Building, which includes Clapp Recital Hall and Harper Hall. Next in line, side by side, are the University Theatre Building (which houses E.C. Mabie Theatre, where student productions are staged), the Museum of Art and the Art Building.

The Johnson County Landmark Jazz Band has won the overall award at the Notre Dame Jazz Festival several years and has scored well in European events. The band was a featured act at the 1983 Montreux Jazz Festival, the world's most famous jazz fest, held in Montreux, Switzerland. Performances of the Stradivari Quartet, formerly the Iowa Quartet, receive kudos everywhere. Members are on the faculty of the School of Music.

Owen and Leone Elliott of Cedar Rapids triggered the building of the Museum of Art in 1962 when they offered the University their extensive art collection if a museum were built to house and display it. More than 2,000 individuals and businesses contributed $1.2 million. In 1976, Roy J. Carver made a gift which enabled the Carver Wing to be added, bringing the exhibition space to 48,000 square feet.

The Art Museum holds a trove of treasures. More than 5,000 objects are in the permanent collections. Included are the Elliott Collections of prints and paintings, English silver and rare Oriental jade. The Stanley Collection of African Sculpture is outstanding. It is a promised gift of Mr. and Mrs. C. Maxwell Stanley of Muscatine, Iowa. Prints and drawings by Mauricio Lasansky are displayed in the Lasansky Room.

The Eve Drewelowe Gallery in the Art Building is a showcase for art work by students and visiting artists.

Iowa was one of the first universities to hire established artists as professors, beginning with Grant Wood.

Mauricio Lasansky joined the Department of Art and Art History in 1945, establishing a printmaking workshop of world fame. Printmakers Virginia Myers and Keith Achepohl continue the tradition.

Artistic resources located elsewhere on campus include Dance, Writers' Workshop, International Writing Program, Film and the Windhover Press, where fine books are handcrafted.

In the summers of 1982 and 1983, the Joffrey II dancers, apprentice group of the Joffrey Ballet, spent residencies on the UI campus under the sponsorship of the National Endowment for the Arts, Hancher Auditorium and corporate and individual gifts. Thanks to the success of the first two Joffrey II residencies, Iowa Dance Residencies program has been established for ongoing summer residencies by dance companies.

Stone ornamentation, Macbride Hall.

Paul Engle

In the 1920s, Iowa pioneered the idea of accepting creative works for thesis credit in the fine arts. In 1932, Paul Engle was one of the first to receive an M.A. in creative writing. His collection of poems, *Worn Earth*, won the Yale Younger Poets prize.

Iowa's famous Writers' Workshop began in 1936 with Wilbur Schramm as its head. Prof. Engle succeeded him in 1941, and although retired, is a tireless raiser of funds to provide scholarships for budding writers.

For almost 50 years, the workshop has drawn students, teachers and lecturers of talent. A partial list includes Kurt Vonnegut, Jr., Flannery O'Connor, Robert Penn Warren, Robert Frost, Philip Roth, John Irving, Nelson Algren, Donald Justice, John Cheever, Vance Bourjaily, Gail Godwin, Curtis Harnack, James A. McPherson, W.D. Snodgrass, Robert Lowell and Wallace Stegner. James Michener was so impressed with the program that he gave the University a $500,000 trust fund for annual awards to American prose writers attending the workshop.

The International Writing Program, first directed by Prof. Engle and now under the direction of his wife, Hualing Nieh Engle, attracts writers from all over the world. UI also offers a Translation Workshop.

Fine Print

Since Kim Merker founded The University of Iowa's Windhover Press in 1967, he has printed unpublished works by such distinguished authors as George Bernard Shaw, Henry David Thoreau and W.H. Auden.

He prints limited editions of original material, setting type by hand and printing on flatbed hand presses over a century old on paper handmade in Europe and Japan. The sheets are then folded, gathered, sewn and put into cases by hand.

The Windhover Press has won several prestigious awards from the American Institute of Graphic Arts.

Each semester Prof. Merker apprentices six to eight students, teaching them the techniques of hand printing in the Windhover Press workshop.

Iowa City's rich heritage of small presses dates back to 1945 when Carroll Coleman founded the UI's typography laboratory in the School of Journalism and directed his Prairie Press. Harry Duncan, director of the Cummington Press, succeeded him from 1955 to 1972. Their students tended to settle nearby, and there may be more small presses per capita in the Iowa City area than any other place in America. Included are the Corycian Press, the Penumbra Press, the Seamark Press, the Toothpaste Press and the Stone Wall Press. A number of others that started in Iowa City have migrated to other parts of the country, where they carry on the Iowa tradition.

Hancher Auditorium
Photo on back cover

Designed by the architects of Lincoln Center and the U.N. building, beautiful Hancher Auditorium is considered one of the best multipurpose performance halls in the nation. Fulfilling the dream of Virgil M. Hancher, president of the University from 1940 to 1964, the 2,684-seat auditorium was built to serve the needs of both the art forms and the arts audience.

Hancher is both an arts resource for the region and a valuable part of the educational process at the University. Since it opened in 1972, Hancher has presented the full spectrum of the arts, from distinguished classical performers such as Vladimir Horowitz, Rudolf Nureyev, Itzhak Perlman and Luciano Pavarotti to touring Broadway shows such as "A Chorus Line" and "Annie."

But Hancher is also the home of student ensembles such as the University Symphony Orchestra, The University of Iowa Opera Theater and the Symphony Band. Each season, students in the fine arts receive valuable experience on the Hancher stage, while students in arts management and technical theater fields learn their crafts working in all aspects of the operation of the auditorium, from the box office to the food service to backstage.

The list of world-famous celebrities who have performed in Hancher includes Dizzy Gillespie, Beverly Sills, Victor Borge, Marcel Marceau, the Joffrey Ballet, Charles Treger, Phyllis Diller, Leontyne Price, Patrice Munsel, Carlos Montoya, Bill Cosby, Artur Rubinstein, Vladimir Ashkenazy, André Watts, Isaac Stern, Joan Sutherland, Andrés Segovia, Ella Fitzgerald, Ferrante and Teicher, and Edward Villella.

Guided tours of Hancher Auditorium are available Wednesdays and Sundays at 2 p.m. while the University is in session.

Those who contribute to Hancher Circle for the Performing Arts through The University of Iowa Foundation receive seating consideration for performances and also receive Hancher Circle publications.

University Theatre
Photo on page 41

University Theatre is one of several buildings clustered on the west bank of the Iowa River forming the Iowa Center for the Arts. It houses the Division of Theatre Arts of the Department of Communication and Theatre Arts and E.C. Mabie Theatre, which showcases work of theater students. Prof. Mabie was director of the University Theatre from 1933 to his death in 1956 and head of the Department of Speech and Dramatic Arts, 1923-56. He played a leading role in establishing the internationally known speech clinic at the University. The theater building was built in 1935 on land reclaimed from the Iowa River by WPA workers in the early 1930s.

High Steppers
Photo on page 46

The "show band" concept for UI's marching band brought everyone to attention in 1954 when Director Frederick C. Ebbs came on the scene. He put the all-male band through its paces for 13 years. In 1974 the band went coed and now the sexes are about equally numbered in the 300-member group.

Promenade

On a boulder behind Iowa Memorial Union is a plaque that reads: *"The founders of Iowa City envisioned a promenade along this bank of the Iowa River. In accordance with their 1839 plat this walk has been so designated by the University of Iowa. 1977."*

A paved walk now follows the river from the south end of the Union (breaking for the intake building of the City Water Works and resuming by North Hall) to the Hancher footbridge. Bikers, joggers and strollers can pause and commune with nature—and with the flock of mallards swimming along the east bank of the river.

University Hospitals

Photos on pages 1, 43 and 44-45

At University Hospitals and Clinics they do what all the king's horses and all the king's men couldn't do for Humpty Dumpty—they put broken (and ailing) bodies back together again.

Much of what they do could be labeled miracles, miracles that happen on an almost daily basis—wonders like open heart surgery, treatment of severe burns, cornea transplants.

What's more, they teach and train others to perform more medical miracles. It's the largest university-owned teaching hospital in the world. And they constantly research ways to help people live longer and healthier lives.

It's Iowa's tertiary care hospital, which means they get the really tough cases, the ones community hospitals aren't equipped to handle. It also means they specialize, with more "ologies" than you can shake a thermometer at—neurology, hematology, endocrinology, otolaryngology—91 of them in all.

Doctors, many of them internationally famous in their specialties, come from all over the world to contribute to this outstanding medical facility.

All of this goes on in a conglomeration of buildings that fills a four-block area on the west campus. When General Hospital was built in the late 1920s, its Gothic tower dominated the scene. Today, the famous landmark blends in with the newer buildings in the Health Science complex.

In the 1970s, a $184 million expansion and upgrading of facilities began, receiving a boost from the $2 million gift of the late Roy J. Carver.

The complex now includes the Psychiatric Hospital; the Steindler Building (formerly Children's Hospital); the Colleges of Medicine, Dentistry, Nursing and Pharmacy; Bowen Science Building; the Health Sciences Library; the University Hospital School and Student Health Service.

Additional medical facilities are located on the 525-acre Oakdale campus, five miles northwest of the Health Center.

Resources, personnel and services are shared with the Veterans Administration Medical Center nearby on Highway 6.

For Iowans, getting to and from the hospitals is a breeze with a unique transportation system that includes the Air-Care Emergency Helicopter service with a landing pad on the hospital roof and 15 automotive vehicles that travel two million miles a year, taking patients to the hospital (and home again).

Benefactor

Between 1971 and his death in 1982, Roy J. Carver, Muscatine industrialist, gave $10 million to the University—a record unmatched by any other contributor. He made his fortune in Bandag, Inc., a tire-retreading company, which he founded in 1957.

Hands On

Children walk up to the display of bronze hands in a hallway at University Hospital and compare the size of their hands with those of Wilt Chamberlain or Van Cliburn.

The castings were made by Dr. Adrian Flatt, a former professor of anatomy and orthopedic surgery at UI and inventor of the artificial finger joint.

Also displayed are the bronzed hand-castings of musicians Isaac Stern and Arthur Fiedler and athletes Stan Musial, Arnold Palmer and Joe DiMaggio.

Presidents Truman, Eisenhower, Johnson and Ford are included, as are ten American astronauts and scientist Werner Von Braun.

Johnson County residents gathered at Old Capitol in 1865 for a memorial service after President Lincoln was assassinated.

Old Capitol

As the Eiffel Tower is to Paris and the Acropolis is to Athens, so is Old Capitol to Iowa City—a symbol, a landmark, a proud possession.

Iowa's most historic building, Old Capitol was the Territorial Capitol from 1842 to 1846 and the first Iowa State Capitol from 1846 to 1857. When the state government moved to Des Moines, Old Capitol became the first permanent building of the University of Iowa campus. The Greek Revival building and 10 acres of land were given to the school by the state.

Designed by John F. Rague, Old Capitol took 14 years to build. The unfinished building was first used in 1842 by the Territorial Legislature. Most of the Devonian limestone came from the banks of the Iowa River near North Liberty. It was floated down the river on rafts, then pulled by oxen to "Capitol Square." Handhewn native trees were also used in the construction. Foundation walls are six feet thick.

Old Capitol was renovated from 1921 to 1924 and restored from 1972 to 1976. Although included in the original plans, the west portico was not built until the 1920s. At that time, gold leaf five-millionths of an inch thick was added to the copper-covered dome. Steel supporting beams replaced many of the original oak beams.

In the 1972-76 restoration of Old Capitol, three eras are represented, a novel approach. The Senate Chamber and the President's Office, reflecting the 1920s, honor the 110 years the University used the building. Since the mid-1860s, every president through Willard Boyd had his office in Old Capitol.

The other two eras defined in the Old Capitol restoration are 1842-46, the territorial period, and 1846-57, the period that Iowa City was the state capital.

Prof. Margaret Keyes was director of research and Mrs. Virgil M. Hancher, chairman of the restoration committee.

Old Capitol, a National Historic Landmark, is open for tours Monday-Saturday 10 a.m. to 3 p.m. and Sunday noon to 4 p.m. without charge. On football Saturdays, hours are 9 a.m. to noon.

The stories Old Capitol could tell! Its memories go back to 1842, even before Iowa was a state, back to the four years it was the Capitol of the Territory of Iowa when early settlers debated, argued and pleaded as they carved a state out of the wilderness.

Inside its sturdy walls, the territorial government had its offices, the territorial Supreme Court struggled to make the right decisions, the first State Constitution was drafted, the first governor of the State of Iowa was inaugurated, the State Historical Society was formed, the Iowa Republican Party was born.

Through the years, political rallies made its rafters ring with speeches, cheers and grand ideas. Herbert Hoover spoke from its steps as a candidate.

Here the state government operated from 1846 to 1857 before moving to Des Moines. Now Old Capitol heard the sounds of young voices reciting in class-rooms. It heard lectures and chapel ser-vices and housed the first University li-brary, the College of Law and an Armory.

Generations of students heeded the tolling of its bell as they hurried to classes. And it still tolls.

That bell rang three days and three nights in respect for Abraham Lincoln in 1865 when the news of his assassination reached Iowa City. Old Capitol looked on as mourners gathered for a service in memory of their fallen leader. The scene was reenacted almost a hundred years later in 1963 when another crowd grieved for John F. Kennedy.

Periodically, the shadows of war fell across Old Capitol. During the Civil War, army officers recruited students on Old Capitol's lawn. To dramatize the war ef-fort during World War I, President Jessup tore a piece of wood from Old Capitol and sent it to Washington, D.C., to be burned in a Liberty Loan bonfire. Khaki and navy dotted the campus from 1942 to 1945 when 36,357 servicemen trained at UI during World War II.

Another war brought other kinds of re-actions. In 1970, about 1,000 demonstra-tors protesting the Vietnam War met in front of Old Capitol. From across Clinton Street came the sounds of breaking glass as rocks were thrown through store windows.

There were happy scenes, too—June fêtes; Commencement services; Alumni reunions; Fourth of July celebrations with brass bands and patriotic speeches; Homecoming bonfires, pep rallies and corn monuments; solemn Induction Ser-vices for new students in the fall and tap-ping of Mortar Board candidates in the spring.

In 1939, Iowa City celebrated its cen-tennial with a pageant on Old Capitol's steps. B.F. Shambaugh, head of the Politi-cal Science Department and superinten-dent of the State Historical Society of Iowa, read the prologue, and the Rev. James Waery spoke as the Voice of Old Capitol.

On Gentle Thursday, May 11, 1967, stu-dent "flower children," bedecked with beads, gamboled on the Pentacrest lawn, giving out kisses, balloons, candy and baked banana peels (said to be hallucino-genic), flying kites, singing and paying homage to guest-of-honor poet Allen Ginsberg.

Old Capitol watched Hare Krishna dis-ciples with shaved heads and saffron robes sit on the Pentacrest lawn, chanting and trying to convert passing students. It saw a nuclear disarmament march, and it saw women carrying "Women Take Back the Night" signs in an anti-rape demon-stration.

Old Capitol saw the student body swell from a roomful of students to nearly 30,000 and saw new buildings mushroom in all directions, changing dramatically its western view of the meandering Iowa River and the gently rolling prairie.

For the University, there have been good times and bad, peaceful times and violent. Each fall, a new crop of students descends on the campus, replacing those who marched off in the spring, diplomas firmly clutched in eager hands. Each dec-ade brings new buildings, new students, new professors to add their strength to the University. Old Capitol looks on calm-ly and serenely. Its dominant spirit lives on.

Solid black walnut desks and chairs in the House Chamber of Old Capitol are replicas of those used by legislators in the 1840s and 1850s. The furniture was made by Schanz Furniture Shop of South Amana, Iowa. The carpet is a reproduction of a mid-nineteenth century Brussels carpet. Quill pens are reproductions, but the brass candlesticks are antiques. Candles are hand-dipped tallow candles made by Louise Pauley of Iowa City. She and her husband, the late Glenn Pauley, made candles used throughout the building as a gift for the opening in 1976, and she continues to provide them. The flag is a reproduction of a 29-star flag of 1846 with a large star in the center representing Iowa. The speaker's chair and the two desks and side chairs on the platform are original.

Three justices would sit at a bench such as this in the Supreme Court Chamber on the first floor of the restored Old Capitol. It is an approximation of what the restoration committee gleaned from its study of other state capitols. The two desk tables with leather inserts and the four firehouse Windsor chairs of the 1840s would be for the defense and prosecution. Authentic law books opened on the desks give the impression that the pioneer lawyers have just stepped out of the room for a recess. The ceiling light fixture, one of a pair in the room, is a Tole whale-oil chandelier (circa 1830), the type used in those days. The chandeliers have been electrified, but have never been refinished. An astral lamp is on either end of the bench. Between the desks is one of the ceramic Bennington-style spittoons found throughout the building.

This pine bookcase in the Territorial-State Library on the first floor of Old Capitol was in place in 1857 and may be original to the building. It holds part of the original collection of books, of which over a thousand have been found. The books came from the Iowa Historical Library in Des Moines and from individuals. The committee used the two earliest catalogs of the collection in their search for the old books and were helped by the fact that each book in the original collection was labeled "Iowa State Library" on the bottom of page 30. Walnut side chairs and drop-leaf tables are circa 1845, and walnut armchairs are circa 1855. The tables are covered with green baize. Portable library steps for the librarian to use in reaching top shelves are by the bookcase. On the floor is an ingrain carpet of the period.

Above: English-Philosophy Building and Main Library

Above: Zoology Building
Below: Lindquist Center
Middle right: Van Allen Hall
Bottom right: Phillips Hall

Red banners draped from the Ionic columns of Macbride Hall's east portico announce the Museum of Natural History's Iowa Hall campaign.
Below: University Theatre

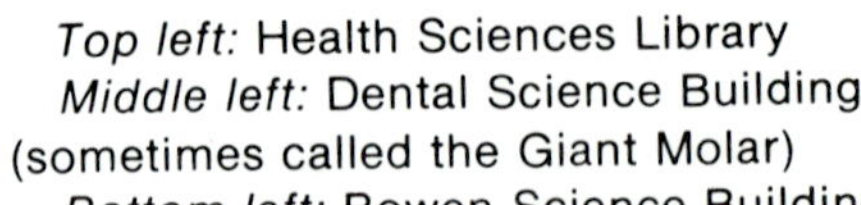

Top left: Health Sciences Library
Middle left: Dental Science Building
(sometimes called the Giant Molar)
Bottom left: Bowen Science Building
Below: Pharmacy Building
Below bottom: Nursing Building

Top right: A new main entrance to The University of Iowa Hospitals and Clinics was opened in 1978. The well-manicured landscape features a large fountain and a sculpture, *Folded Square Alphabet D.*

Bottom right: The East Courtyard of the John W. Colloton Pavilion provides an outdoor area for the enjoyment of patients, visitors and staff. Opened in the fall of 1982, the Colloton Pavilion houses the Iowa Children's Health Care Center, which is reflected in the wall of energy-saving, mirrored windows.

Following pages: A football Saturday afternoon in Iowa City. Jim Kent photograph.

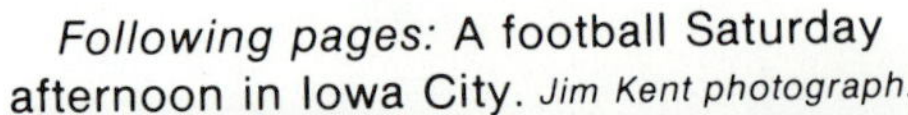

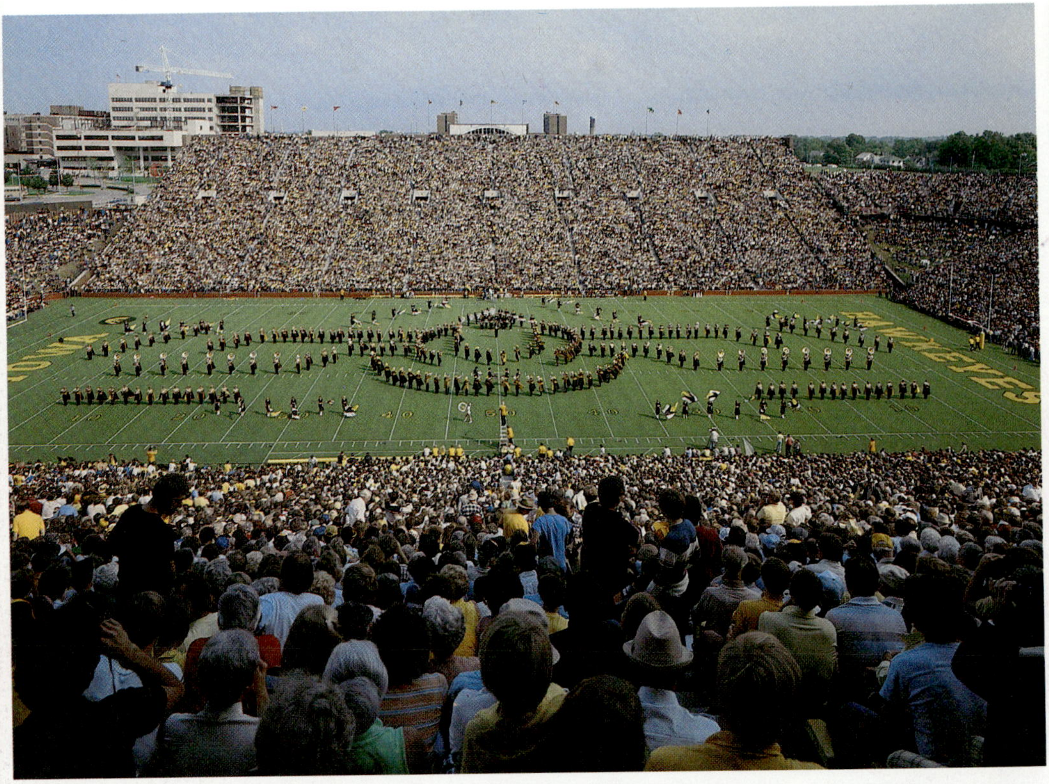

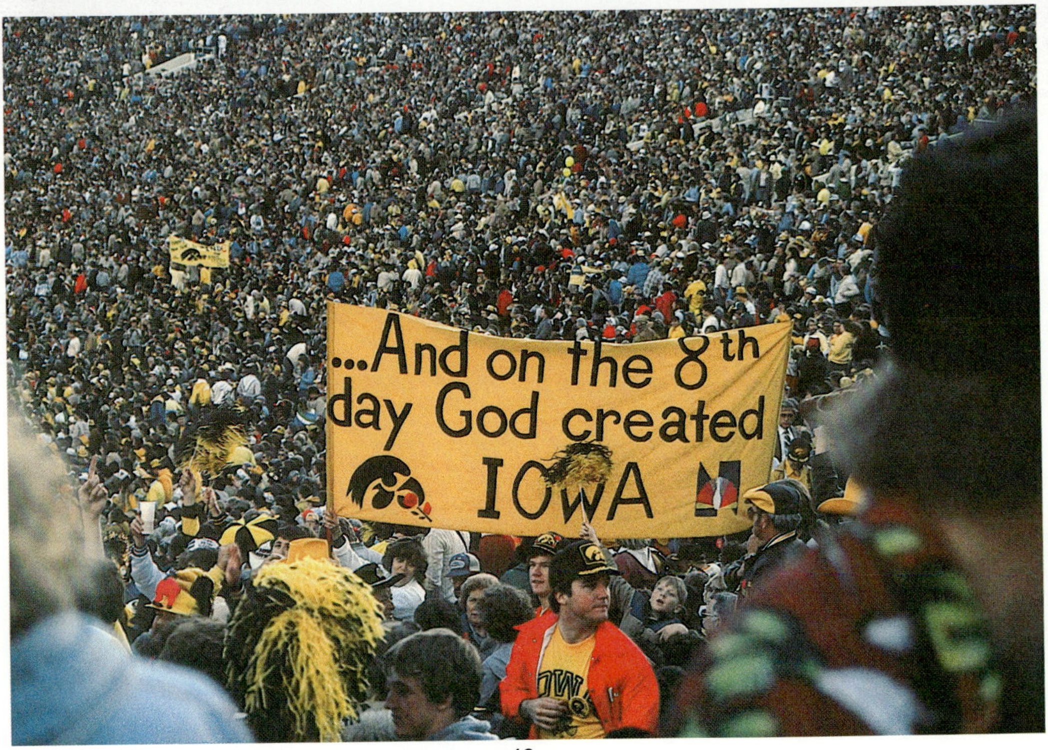

...And on the 8th
day God created
IOWA

Top left: Performing at halftime is The University of Iowa Hawkeye Marching Band of about 300 members.

Bottom left: University of Iowa fans hoisted this sign at the Rose Bowl, Pasadena, California, during the 1982 New Year's Day game.

Above: The Carver-Hawkeye Arena, opened in 1983, is used for basketball, wrestling, volleyball, gymnastics, tennis, concerts and other University functions.

Right: Herky the Hawk on the right and football's Tiger Hawk on the left.

Early postcards show the Field House, top, built in 1927, and the Iowa Memorial Union, bottom, as it looked from 1926 to 1955.

Above: This historic postcard is of the former home of the University Hospital on the east side of the campus. The building complex later became known as East Hall to several generations of students. Today it is Seashore Hall.

Below: This postcard of Currier Hall, circa 1915, shows the women's dormitory long before additional dorms were built nearby.

Quadrangle Dormitory,
State University of Iowa,
Iowa City, Iowa

6B716-N

An early postcard of the Quadrangle
Dormitory is above, while Hillcrest is
shown reflected in the Iowa River,
bottom postcard.

Above: Danforth Chapel, a replica of an 1874 country church, is on the east bank of the Iowa River near the Iowa Memorial Union.

Below: Students cross the footbridge near the School of Music and Hancher Auditorium to Stanley Hall and the other east-side dorms.

This decorative fountain, donated by the Class of 1936, marks the entrance to the scenic footbridge linking the Iowa Memorial Union with the arts complex.

The limestone-rimmed pond across from the School of Art and Art History on Riverside Drive is a favorite campus landmark.

Appetizers

Mexican Dip

Jean Lloyd-Jones serves in the Iowa Legislature as a state representative from Iowa City. She received her master's degree in history from UI. Her husband, Richard, is director of the School of Letters and chairman of the English Department.

3 medium-sized ripe avocados
2 Tbsp. lemon juice
½ tsp. salt
¼ tsp. pepper
1 cup sour cream
1 pkg. taco seasoning mix
  mayonnaise
2 10-oz. cans plain or jalapeño bean
  dip
1 cup chopped green onion and tops
3 medium tomatoes, chopped (about
  2 cups)
2 4½-oz. cans chopped ripe olives
1 4-oz. pkg. shredded sharp Cheddar
  cheese
  tortilla chips for dipping

Peel and mash avocados with lemon juice, salt and pepper. In a bowl combine sour cream, taco seasoning mix and enough mayonnaise to spread easily.

To assemble, spread bean dip in shallow serving platter; top with seasoned avocado mixture, then with sour cream mixture. Sprinkle with chopped onion, tomatoes and olives. Cover with cheese. Serve chilled with chips. Serves 10 to 20. Can be prepared in advance.

Liptauer Cheese

Mary Bryant, Iowa City, is a volunteer in the Old Capitol Gift Shop. Her husband, Donald, is a professor emeritus in the Department of Communication and Theatre Arts and was a Carver Distinguished Professor.

Liptauer is a German-style cream cheese and butter mixture for spreading on crackers.

1 8-oz. pkg. cream cheese
½ cup softened butter or margarine
½ cup commercial sour cream
½ tsp. dry mustard
2 tsp. capers
2 Tbsp. anchovy paste
¼ cup minced green onion
2 tsp. paprika
1 Tbsp. caraway seed

Combine all ingredients in blender. Makes about two cups.

Shrimp Dip

Elizabeth Stanley, Muscatine, shares with her husband, Maxwell, the joy of collecting African art. The Stanley Collection in The University of Iowa Museum of Art contains 180 African objects. The Stanley Foundation promotes world peace.

1 4½-oz. can small shrimp, rinsed and
  drained
¼ cup yogurt or milk
1 8-oz. pkg. cream cheese, at room
  temperature
1 Tbsp. lemon juice
1 tsp. Worcestershire sauce
½ tsp. garlic salt
¼ tsp. dill weed

Mash shrimp with fork and add yogurt or milk. Blend in cream cheese. Stir in lemon juice, Worcestershire sauce, garlic salt and dill weed. Store in covered container in refrigerator. Makes about 1½ cups.

This freezes well and is delicious spread on sliced rounds of small zucchini or as a dip with crisp celery.

Editor's Note: *Most of these recipes were contributed especially for* On Iowa. *Others were selected from the* Old Capitol Cookbook, *published in 1978 by Old Capitol volunteers and no longer in print. Those recipes are included in this book with the permission of the contributors.*

Hot Crabmeat Dip

Lee Wockenfuss is married to James Wockenfuss, director of Hancher Auditorium.

1 8-oz. pkg. cream cheese
½ cup butter
1 small onion, finely chopped
3 or 4 dashes Tabasco sauce
    red pepper, to taste
1 clove garlic, pressed
16 to 18 oz. white crabmeat, thawed if
    frozen, well drained

In top of double boiler, melt cream cheese and butter. Stir in onion, seasonings and garlic. Add crabmeat, mix thoroughly and heat. Serve hot in chafing dish with assorted crackers.

"This is easy, delicious and versatile," Lee explains. "I have also served it on small phyllo pastry squares, in pastry shells, as a stuffing for mushrooms, with fresh asparagus as a crêpe filling and in a number of other ways. It's one of those recipes that is so easy you almost hate to admit it!"

Party Snacks

Helen E. Focht, Iowa City.

1 10-oz. pkg. sharp Cheddar cheese
1 12-oz. pkg. Jimmy Dean's hot
    sausage
3 cups Bisquick

Melt cheese. Break up sausage with fork and add to cooled cheese. Add Bisquick. Mix well with hands. Make into walnut-sized balls. Bake on a cookie sheet at 350° about 20 minutes. Roll balls around once or twice to get them browned on all sides. Makes about 50 or 60.

These can be prepared ahead of time by freezing them on a cookie sheet and then placing them in a plastic bag in the freezer. Defrost before baking.

Fried Won Ton

Pearl Zemlicka, Iowa City, has worked more than 400 hours as a docent at Old Capitol. She is a retired faculty member of the College of Nursing.

1 cup ground pork (or chicken, shrimp
    or other meat)
1 Tbsp. minced onion
1 tsp. pulverized garlic
    dash pepper
    dash monosodium glutamate
1 egg plus 1 yolk
1 pkg. won ton skins (4-in. squares)
1 egg white to seal won tons
2 cups vegetable oil
    chopped water chestnuts or
    mushrooms (optional)

Mix first six ingredients in a bowl. Place about ¾ teaspoon of mixture in center of each skin. Wet edges with egg white, fold into a triangle and seal edges tightly. Pinch together with two opposite ends on the folded side. Drop in hot fat, about 375°, and fry until brown on all sides. Drain on paper towel. These freeze nicely. Fry as you need them. Chopped water chestnuts or mushrooms may be added to meat mixture if desired. Serve with Sweet and Sour Sauce.

Sweet and Sour Sauce:
1 cup sugar
¼ cup cider vinegar
1 tsp. salt
½ cup water
2½ Tbsp. catsup (or more)
1 to 2 Tbsp. cornstarch mixed with
    small amount of water

Put sugar, vinegar, salt, water and catsup in small pot and bring to a boil. Add cornstarch dissolved in water; stir and cook until sauce is thick and clear. Remove from heat. Use with either egg rolls or won ton.

Russian Borscht

Mary Meis Collins, a graduate of UI, and her husband, Arthur Collins, live in Dallas, Texas. In Cedar Rapids, Iowa, Arthur founded the internationally known Collins Radio Company, which was purchased in 1973 by Rockwell International Corporation. Mary says this dish was served at a "Foods of the Allied Nations" supper at UI by the Home Economics Department in 1943.

1 lb. lean beef, cubed
1 soup bone
1 chicken, cut up
3 carrots, chopped
3 small onions, sliced
3 stalks celery, diced
3 qts. water
¼ tsp. peppercorns
½ bay leaf
1 spray thyme
1 sprig parsley
   salt and pepper
2 uncooked beets, chopped
   sour heavy cream

Put beef, soup bone, chicken, carrots, onions, celery and water in large kettle and bring slowly to a boil. Tie spices and herbs in a small cloth bag; add with parsley to soup mixture and simmer, covered, for 2 hours.

Strain and season soup to taste. Add beets and cook 15 minutes; strain and reheat. Serve with a topping of whipped sour cream. Serves 8-10.

Gazpacho

Eloise January shares many interests with her husband, Dr. Lewis January, professor emeritus of internal medicine at The University of Iowa. A major interest is professional ballet. Dr. January is a member of the board of directors of the Joffrey Ballet Company.

3 lbs. tomatoes, peeled and seeded, or
   6 cups canned Italian tomatoes
1 onion
½ cucumber, peeled and seeded
1 clove garlic
2 cups tomato juice
½ tsp. cumin
   salt and freshly ground pepper
¼ cup olive oil
¼ cup white wine vinegar
To accompany gazpacho:
   garlic croutons
½ cup chopped green or Spanish onion
½ cup chopped green pepper
½ cup chopped cucumber
½ cup chopped fresh tomatoes

Mix tomatoes, onion, cucumber and garlic in blender and process until smooth. Add tomato juice, cumin, salt and pepper. Chill. Before serving, add olive oil and vinegar. Serve in soup bowls. In separate serving bowls put croutons, onion, green pepper, cucumber and tomatoes to pass at the table.

"An excellent first course," Eloise says.

Zucchini Soup

Ulfert Wilke is a distinguished artist known for his calligraphic studies. He was the first director of The University of Iowa Museum of Art.

3 to 4 medium zucchini
2 medium onions, coarsely chopped
    tarragon, fresh or freeze-dried,
      chopped
    chicken stock
2 to 3 Tbsp. instant farina
    sour cream, heavy cream or
      half-and-half

Scrub zucchini and cut into chunks. Sauté onion in butter until soft and transparent but not brown. Add zucchini to onion; add a *little* water and simmer until zucchini is soft.

Purée vegetables in blender or food processor. Add tarragon. Mixture can be frozen at this point.

To the purée, add chicken stock (fresh, homemade or canned) until soup is thinned out. Bring to boil. Thicken with farina sprinkled on boiling soup. Stir until thick.

Add sour cream, heavy cream or half-and-half until it reaches the consistency desired. Add salt, pepper and additional chopped tarragon to taste.

This soup can be served hot or chilled.

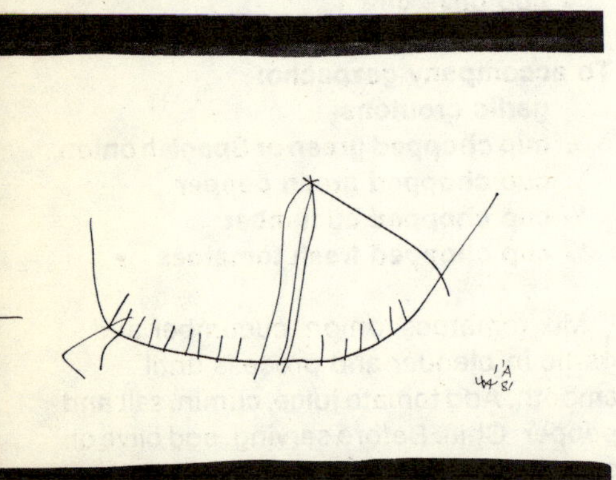

Viking Ship (1981), an ink and water-color drawing by Ulfert Wilke, one of a series on that subject done in a spare, calligraphic style.

Cream of Broccoli Soup

Lucy Broadston is athletic fund-raiser for the Women's Athletic Department. It was a newly created position when she accepted it in 1978. This recipe is one that Lucy invented herself.

⅓ cup butter
⅓ cup flour
1 14-oz. can chicken broth
1 pt. half-and-half
1 1-lb. bag frozen cut broccoli spears
    (flowerettes)
    salt and pepper to taste
    dash of nutmeg

Melt butter until bubbly. Stir in flour. Cook about a minute. Add broth and half-and-half all at once. Stir constantly until thick and bubbly. Add seasonings. Turn heat to simmer. Add broccoli. Cover and heat through about half an hour until broccoli is tender; don't let mixture boil.

Breads

Grape-Nuts Bread

Bonnie Brechler of Iowa City helped write the Old Capitol Cookbook *and has worked in the Old Capitol Gift Shop. She is the housemother for Alpha Phi sorority.*

- 2 cups buttermilk
- 1 cup Grape-Nuts cereal
- 1½ cups sugar
- ¼ tsp. salt
- 2 eggs
- 4 cups flour
- 2 tsp. baking powder
- 1 tsp. soda

Pour buttermilk over Grape-Nuts. Let stand a few minutes. Add sugar, salt and eggs; beat well. Sift flour, baking powder and soda together. Add to other ingredients and beat well. Bake in two greased 9x5-inch pans at 350° for 50 minutes or until tester comes out clean.

Pumpkin Bread

Judy Richmond Brown, Iowa City.

- 3 cups flour
- 2 Tbsp. baking powder
- 2 tsp. baking soda
- 1 tsp. salt
- 1 Tbsp. cinnamon
- 4 eggs
- 2 cups sugar
- 2 cups (1-lb. can) cooked pumpkin
- 1¼ cups cooking oil

Blend the flour, baking powder, baking soda, salt and cinnamon. Set mixture aside. Beat the eggs. Blend the sugar into the beaten eggs. Add pumpkin and oil to egg and sugar mixture. Blend in the flour mixture. Pour into two greased 9x5-inch loaf pans. Bake at 350° for 50 to 60 minutes. Bread is done when toothpick inserted into center comes out clean. Bread can be made ahead and frozen until it is needed.

Sour Milk Brown Bread

Mary Ellen Comly, North Liberty, has served on the North Liberty City Council and Planning and Zoning Commission.

- 2 cups sour milk
- 2 level tsp. soda (dissolved in milk)
- pinch salt
- ¾ cup sugar
- 2 Tbsp. molasses
- 2 cups graham flour
- 1 cup white flour
- ⅓ cup chopped nuts
- ⅓ cup raisins, chopped if you wish

Combine ingredients in order given. Bake in large loaf pan or two small ones at 350° for 45 to 60 minutes. Do not double recipe.

Herb Bread

Dottie Klein Ray, Iowa City, was editor of the Daily Iowan *in 1944-45. She began a live daily interview program, "The Dottie Ray Show," over radio station KXIC in 1957. Her husband, the late Dr. Robert F. Ray, was dean of the Division of Continuing Education. He was a Big Ten and NCAA faculty representative for 26 years. "Cooking is not my long suit," Dottie confesses, "but this recipe goes with everything and is a nice change from garlic bread."*

- 1 lb. butter or margarine, melted
- 2 tsp. basil
- 2 tsp. thyme
- 1½ tsp. sage
- 2 tsp. marjoram
- 4 Tbsp. minced chives
- 2 loaves commercial French bread

Mix together all of ingredients for spread. Slice loaves of French bread 4/5 through; then brush mixture on both sides of each slice. Wrap loaves in foil and heat at 350° for 15 minutes.

May 1935 archery class near the Art Building.

Cream Scones

Mary Ellen Comly of North Liberty, a volunteer at Old Capitol, shares a recipe for scones, a delicacy the British love to team up with their afternoon tea.

2 cups flour
3 tsp. baking powder
½ tsp. salt
4 Tbsp. sugar, divided
6 Tbsp. shortening
2 eggs
½ cup light cream or evaporated milk

Have ingredients at room temperature. Sift flour and measure; add baking powder, salt and half of the sugar; sift again. Add shortening and cut in until mixture is like meal. Beat eggs slightly with fork; stir in milk or cream. Reserve 2 teaspoons and pour rest into flour mixture. Stir until just mixed. Turn out on lightly floured board. Knead dough lightly for about ½ minute, then roll into 7x14-inch rectangle. Brush with reserved egg mixture and sprinkle evenly with remaining sugar. Cut into 3½-inch squares (or smaller, if preferred), then in half diagonally to make triangles. With spatula place on ungreased cookie sheet. Bake at 450° until lightly browned, 8 to 10 minutes. Serve hot. Makes 16 scones.

These freeze well and are easy to defrost and heat, either in a microwave or conventional oven, so a double recipe can be made.

Banana Bran Pancakes

Nancy Seiberling, North Liberty, Iowa, is a founder of the much-honored Project Green, which has been beautifying Iowa City and its environs since 1968. "I have long been interested in gardening—and in bringing nature into the kitchen for adventures in cooking. This is an original recipe, intended to produce a delicious and really nutritious breakfast treat. Sunflower seeds and unprocessed bran used in this recipe may be purchased at food co-ops and health food stores."

Nancy's husband, Frank A. Seiberling, was director of the School of Art and Art History from 1959 to 1976.

1 egg, beaten
¾ cup buttermilk
¾ cup mashed banana
2 Tbsp. honey or brown sugar
4 Tbsp. melted butter
¾ cup whole wheat flour
½ tsp. soda
1 tsp. baking powder
¼ cup unprocessed bran (not packaged cereal)
¼ cup sunflower seeds (hulled but not roasted or salted)
banana slices, as needed

Beat the egg; add buttermilk, mashed banana, sweetening and butter. To the whole wheat flour, add soda and baking powder and stir into liquids. Add bran and sunflower seeds and mix together, stirring only enough to dampen the flour.

Drop by spoonfuls on buttered hot griddle. On top of each pancake, place three slices of banana while pancake is cooking. When pancake is turned, these will cook enough to provide a delightful flavor. Be sure to butter griddle again before baking the next round of pancakes. This will serve four people, depending on appetites.

Skiing on the Pentacrest, April 1926.

Overnight Coffeecake

Jane Gray, Iowa City. All Homecoming buttons shown in this book are from her collection.

²⁄₃ **cup vegetable oil**
1 **cup white sugar**
½ **cup brown sugar**
2 **eggs**
2 **cups flour**
1 **cup buttermilk or sour milk**
2 **Tbsp. powdered milk**
1 **tsp. baking soda**
1 **tsp. baking powder**
½ **tsp. salt**
1 **tsp. cinnamon**
Topping:
½ **cup brown sugar**
½ **cup chopped nuts**
½ **tsp. cinnamon**

Mix cake ingredients in order given and pour into 13x9-inch baking pan. Combine topping ingredients and sprinkle on top. Cover with plastic wrap or lid and refrigerate overnight.

In the morning, remove wrap or lid and bake at 350° for 30 to 35 minutes.

Good either warm or cold with or without whipped topping.

Spoon Bread

Floy Eugenia Whitehead of Iowa City is professor emeritus and former chairman of the Department of Home Economics.

½ **cup yellow corn meal**
1 **cup water**
¼ **tsp. salt**
2 **Tbsp. butter**
2 **large or 3 small eggs**
½ **cup milk**

Cook corn meal in salted water until stiff. Stir constantly over medium heat. Cool mixture in bowl while buttered 1-quart baking dish is heating in oven at 450°. Add butter to mixture, and cream. Add eggs, one at a time, beating each one in well. Add milk and beat. Pour this batter into hot baking dish. Bake 25 minutes at 450°. Serves two or three.

Basic 100% Whole Wheat Bread

Ruth Shambaugh Watkins, Clarinda, Iowa, was editor of Frivol, the popular humor magazine at the University, in 1943-44. Her cartoon figures illustrated the index of the 1945 Hawkeye yearbook. She received a B.A. and an M.A. from UI. She is a free-lance photographer, writer, cartoonist, portrait painter and self-proclaimed "health nut."

Ruth says, "Since my father and grandfather were both millers—and we now live where the first family gristmill was built in 1855—it's natural enough that homemade bread is a well-established family tradition. This is my favorite bread recipe."

- **1 cup warm water (110 to 115°)**
- **2 Tbsp. active dry yeast**
- **1 cup milk, scalded and cooled to 110° (lukewarm)**
- **⅓ cup honey**
- **¼ cup vegetable oil**
- **2 tsp. salt, preferably sea salt**
- **2 eggs, beaten**
- **5½ to 6 cups stone-ground whole wheat flour**

In mixing bowl, dissolve yeast in warm water. Add cooled milk, honey, oil, salt and eggs. Stir in 2½ cups flour. Beat 100 strokes by hand or 3 to 4 minutes with electric mixer. Cover bowl and allow sponge to rise in a warm place until doubled, about 40 to 45 minutes.

Mix in remaining flour, reserving ½ cup for kneading. Turn out onto floured board and knead 8 to 10 minutes or until smooth and elastic. Place in oiled bowl. Turn dough over to oil top. Cover bowl and let rise in warm place until doubled. Punch down. Turn out onto lightly floured board. Shape into 2 loaves and put in greased 8x4-inch bread pans. Cover and let rise until doubled. Bake at 375° for 40 minutes. Remove from pans and cool on racks.

Variations: Either all or half of the recipe can be made into bread sticks. Bake for 20 to 25 minutes. For Wheat Crunch Bread, add 1 cup chopped sunflower seeds or nuts before adding the last portion of flour.

Houska
(A Christmas Bread)

Kay Brown is director of Humanities/ Science News Service, which handles public relations for the University. Her husband, Tom Brown, is executive director of the Alumni Association. Kay's recipe is a family treasure handed down from generation to generation. "It's a tradition in my Czech family for new brides to start a recipe book with hand-copied recipes from her relatives," says Kay. "This is one of them. We always have houska for Christmas breakfast."

- **1 cup milk, scalded**
- **½ cup sugar**
- **½ cup butter or margarine**
- **1 tsp. salt**
- **4 cups flour (or more), divided**
- **1 egg plus 1 egg yolk**
- **1 cake yeast dissolved in ¼ cup warm water**
- **½ cup light or dark raisins**

Optional:
- **¼ cup candied citron or lemon peel**
- **¼ cup candied pineapple peel**
- **¼ cup candied cherries**
- **¼ cup chopped almonds**
- **1 tsp. grated lemon rind**

Scald milk; add sugar, butter and salt and cool to lukewarm. Add 1 cup flour, eggs and yeast mixture. Add raisins and any or all of the optional ingredients. Add remaining flour. Knead lightly until smooth.

Place in greased bowl, cover and let rise in warm place until doubled, 1½ to 2 hours.

Punch down and divide into three parts; roll each part into a long strand. Place three strands on a greased baking sheet. Braid loosely beginning in the middle; tuck ends under; seal well. Cover and let rise until light, 1 to 1½ hours. Bake at 350° for 50 to 60 minutes. When cool, frost with powdered sugar frosting. Can be frozen unfrosted.

Salads

Salad

John Leggett, director of the Writers' Workshop at UI, is the author of four novels and one biography, Ross and Tom. He is also well known in Iowa City as the host of many lively parties for visiting writers.

For me, salad is one of life's few pleasures which is both exquisite and dependable, but by this word "salad" I mean the dish containing only the following ingredients:

Loose leaf lettuce. (I don't know what can be prepared with iceberg lettuce, probably nothing for human consumption. Boston and redleaf lettuce are the only locally available greens which are acceptable for salad.)

A clove of fresh garlic.
Freshly ground pepper.
Dry mustard.
Red wine vinegar.
Good quality French or Italian olive oil.
A small quantity of salt is optional.
Reliable friends suggest salt may be unhealthy and it is surely dispensable.

First, the lettuce must be thoroughly rinsed and dried.

Next, the bowl, preferably a wooden one, is briskly massaged with the garlic clove which has been crushed between the thumb and the bowl. Remove all shreds of garlic from bowl.

The dry lettuce is laid in the bowl and the dressing, or sauce vinaigrette, is prepared in the bowl of the salad spoon or a cup. The ground black pepper and a generous pinch of dry mustard are dissolved in a dollop of red wine vinegar and supplemented by two dollops of olive oil.

The leaves are drenched with the dressing and tossed until each leaf is glossy with it and touched with the kiss of the garlic. The salad is ready to exalt the spirit, but mind—*no* substitutions.

Meredith Willson's Mother's Cole Slaw

Meredith Willson may be better known for composing the words and music to The Music Man, *but he is also composer of the "Iowa Fight Song" for The University of Iowa. When the Hawkeyes went to the Rose Bowl Jan. 1, 1982, Willson conducted the University's marching band in a special rendition of the popular fight song. A native of Mason City, Iowa, Willson at one time played flute with the John Philip Sousa band. He now lives in Los Angeles.*

Willson writes: "I'm happy to share my mother's cole slaw recipe with my fellow Iowans. Mason City and everything and everybody in Iowa will always be close to my heart!"

1 cup apple cider vinegar
1 cup sugar
  salt and pepper to taste
½ cup finely chopped crisp unpeeled
   red apple
  chopped cabbage
6 ice cubes
1 cup heavy cream
  salt to taste
1 tsp. prepared mustard
1 tsp. salad dressing

Mix vinegar and sugar. Add seasonings. Combine apple and cabbage and cover with vinegar mixture, adding ice cubes. Let stand in refrigerator for about 6 hours.

Meanwhile, whip and salt the cream, adding mustard and salad dressing. When ready to serve, squeeze the cabbage mixture, one handful at a time, until it is entirely free of the vinegar juice. Then, just before serving, combine it with the whipped cream mixture, 1 tablespoon at a time, until it is a nice slaw or salad consistency, but not "sloppy."

Moroccan Orange Salad

Larry Eckholt, director of arts fundraising at The University of Iowa Foundation, says, "This recipe comes with gratitude to Paula Wolfert for introducing me to the delights of Moroccan cooking."

- **1 head romaine lettuce**
- **3 navel oranges**
- **¼ cup orange juice, divided**
- **2 Tbsp. freshly squeezed lemon juice**
- **2 Tbsp. sugar**
- **pinch of salt**
- **½ tsp. cinnamon**
- **1 Tbsp. orange flower water***
- **¾ cup chopped walnuts**

Wash lettuce and section the leaves, discarding tough outer ones. Drain and pat dry with paper towels. Chill. Peel oranges, removing outside membranes. Section oranges. Keep moist with 2 tablespoons orange juice. Cover and keep chilled.

Make dressing by mixing lemon juice, sugar, salt, cinnamon, orange flower water and remaining 2 tablespoons orange juice. Blend well. Dressing should be sweet.

Just before serving, shred lettuce and arrange in a glass serving dish. Pour dressing over greens and toss. Line orange sections around edge of dish, overlapping slightly. Sprinkle salad with chopped walnuts and dust with cinnamon. Serve immediately.

A slightly heavier and less sweet salad dressing can be made by adding ¼ cup of the highest quality French olive oil to the lemon juice/orange flower water mixture.

*Orange flower water can be found in most food specialty stores.

Broccoli-Cauliflower Salad

Louane (Jerry) Newsome was a professor in the School of Library Science for 20 years until her retirement in 1973. A docent at Old Capitol since 1976, she says, "I love the building and love to tell people about it."

- **1 small head cauliflower**
- **2 stalks fresh broccoli**
- **2 bunches green onions, finely chopped**

Dressing:
- **¾ cup mayonnaise**
- **¾ cup sour cream**
- **1 Tbsp. sugar**
- **1 Tbsp. vinegar**
- **dash Tabasco sauce**
- **1 Tbsp. Worcestershire sauce**
- **1 Tbsp. salt**

Wash cauliflower and broccoli and break into small flowerettes, using only blossoms of the broccoli. Add onion and cover with dressing. Let stand overnight. Serve in lettuce cups. Serves 8.

For dressing, mix all ingredients together.

Barclay Plantation Spinach Salad

Carol Brandt, Iowa City.

- **8 cups washed spinach leaves**
- **½ cup diced Bermuda onion**
- **½ cup mayonnaise**
- **2 Tbsp. white wine vinegar**
- **¼ cup sugar**
- **¼ cup half-and-half**
- **3 hard-cooked eggs, 2 diced and 1 sliced**
- **½ lb. bacon, fried and crumbled**
- **1 cup garlic-flavored croutons**

Chill spinach leaves for several hours until crisp. In large jar combine onion, mayonnaise, vinegar, sugar, half-and-half and the 2 diced hard-cooked eggs. Shake the jar until dressing is well mixed. Refrigerate while spinach leaves chill.

To serve, place spinach in a large bowl. Pour dressing over greens and toss. Sprinkle the crumbled bacon and croutons over salad. Toss lightly. Decorate with the sliced hard-cooked egg. Serves eight.

Women's track meet in May 1925.

Cooked Dressing

Ann Mercer Feddersen graduated from UI in 1945 and her husband, Dick, in 1942. Ann was a member of Mortar Board, national honorary society for scholarship and leadership. Dick was one of the original Scottish Highlanders, a band of bagpipers and drummers wearing authentic regalia that represented UI beginning in 1937. The Feddersens live in North Liberty. "We have lived in the Iowa City area since our marriage in 1947," Ann says, "and have been enjoying the benefits, privileges, pride and joys of the University ever since."

- 3 Tbsp. flour
- 2 Tbsp. salad oil
- 1 cup boiling water
  juice of 1 lemon
- 2 or 3 egg yolks
- 1 cup salad oil
- 1 Tbsp. salt
  paprika

Blend flour and 2 tablespoons salad oil together in a saucepan. Add boiling water and lemon juice and allow to boil up. Remove from heat. Add egg yolks and stir in. Cool to lukewarm.

Beat in 1 cup salad oil, ¼ cup at a time, making certain the oil is thoroughly incorporated. This may be done in a blender or electric mixer. Add approximately 1 tablespoon salt and enough paprika to color.

"There is no way this can curdle," says Ann.

Fire and Ice Tomatoes

A retired medical librarian from the University, Nina Frohwein is a volunteer at Old Capitol Gift Shop.

- 6 large, firm tomatoes, peeled and quartered
- 1 large green pepper, sliced into strips
- 1 large onion, sliced and separated into rings
- 1 cucumber, pared and sliced (added at serving time)

Dressing:
- ¾ cup vinegar
- 1½ tsp. celery salt
- 1½ tsp. mustard seed
- ½ to 1 tsp. salt
- 1 Tbsp. (or more) sugar
- ⅛ tsp. pepper
- ¼ cup water

Place tomatoes, green pepper and onion in a bowl. Combine dressing ingredients, bring to boil and boil hard for 1 minute. While hot, pour over vegetables. Cover and chill overnight. Before serving, add cucumber slices and mix gently.

Artichoke-Rice Salad

Mary Sue Hockmuth of Iowa City is a docent at Old Capitol. She is the daughter of the late Virgil Hancher, president of the University from 1940 to 1964, and Mrs. Hancher.

- **1 pkg. chicken-flavored rice mix**
- **4 green onions, thinly sliced**
- **½ green pepper, chopped**
- **12 pimiento-stuffed olives, sliced**
- **2 6-oz. jars marinated artichoke hearts**
- **⅓ cup mayonnaise**
- **¾ tsp. curry powder**

Cook rice as directed on package, using half the amount of butter called for. Cool in large bowl. Add onion, pepper and olives. Drain artichokes, reserving marinade. Cut artichoke hearts in quarters. Combine mayonnaise, curry powder and half of marinade. Add artichoke hearts to rice mixture and toss. Chill several hours or overnight. Serves 6 to 8.

Curried Rice Salad

Barbara Stehbens, Iowa City, is an interior designer. Her husband, Jim, is a child psychologist at The University of Iowa Hospitals and Clinics.

- **4 cups chilled cooked rice**
- **2 green peppers, finely chopped**
- **4 Tbsp. drained pimiento, cut in strips**
- **4 Tbsp. raisins**
- **4 Tbsp. chopped parsley**
- **4 Tbsp. chopped green onion**

Dressing:
- **¼ cup olive oil**
- **⅓ cup wine vinegar**
- **1 Tbsp. lemon juice**
- **1 clove garlic, minced**
- **1 Tbsp. sugar**
- **⅛ tsp. curry powder**
- **salt and pepper**

Toss salad ingredients together and chill thoroughly. Combine dressing ingredients and chill.

Just before serving, pour dressing over salad ingredients and toss. Serve on crisp

lettuce. Garnish with tomato wedges. Serves 8.

A good salad to serve with lamb or chicken.

Tomato Aspic Pie

Miriam Rosenbaum Canter served as president of the Hancher Guild, the University Club and University Newcomers. She is a volunteer at Old Capitol.

- **1 envelope unflavored gelatin**
- **¼ cup cold water**
- **1 cup boiling water**
- **2 Tbsp. sugar**
- **1 10-oz. can tomato soup**
- **1 Tbsp. lemon juice**
- **¼ cup chopped green onion**
- **¼ cup chopped green pepper**
- **¼ cup chopped cucumber**
- **1 tsp. dill weed**
- **1 tsp. celery seed**

Crust:
- **1 cup crushed cheese crackers**
- **¼ cup melted butter**

Sprinkle gelatin over cold water to soften. Dissolve in boiling water. Add sugar, soup and lemon juice. Chill until partially set. Stir in chopped vegetables, dill weed and celery seed and mix well. Pour into cheese crust and chill until firm. Serve in wedges. Serves 6 to 8.

To make crust, mix crumbs and melted butter. Press firmly in 8-inch pie plate, building up sides. Bake at 375° for 6 to 7 minutes. Cool before filling.

Entrées

Deep-Dish Enchiladas

Jane Gray is a dyed-in-the-wool Hawkeye fan who was wearing black and gold to Iowa games before it became popular! As an Iowa student, she was in the color guard of the marching band. Each year she carries the University flag to lead the Alumni Band at half-time festivities during the Homecoming football game. She collects Hawkeye memorabilia and owns two complete sets of Homecoming badges.

She and her husband, the late Stuart C. Gray, assistant dean in the College of Education, traditionally entertained after the first Iowa home football game. The guest list started at six in 1960 and grew to more than a hundred. The menu never varied: Margaritas, enchiladas, blueberry muffins, brownies and coffee. "We made the food and started mixing Margaritas Thursday night. Friday night we set up tables and decorated with banners and flags. Saturday we picked up the keg of beer and went to the game. Every year I made a bigger batch of the enchiladas since our guests often brought along their guests. Leftovers are great combined with lettuce, fresh tomatoes, raw onion, grated cheese and small corn chips with a fried egg on top."

1½ lbs. lean ground beef
3 cans enchilada sauce
2 cans refried beans
2 cans water
1 pkg. frozen corn tortillas (12 in package)
3 or 4 medium onions, chopped
1 3-oz. pkg. cream cheese, cut in bits
1 lb. sharp Cheddar cheese, grated
    shredded lettuce for top

Brown hamburger; add enchilada sauce, refried beans and water. Stir until it can be stirred easily (the refried beans are packed solidly and are hard to spread otherwise).

In a small deep roaster pan, layer the unthawed tortillas, hamburger mixture, raw onion, cream cheese and grated cheese until all of the ingredients are used, ending with Cheddar cheese. Bake at 350° until bubbly and the cheese is melted and brown. Serve with lettuce on top and a dollop of sour cream, if desired. Serves 8.

Lasagne

Bobbi Olson is the wife of Iowa's former head basketball coach, Lute Olson. Lute coached at Iowa nine seasons, ending with the 1982-83 season. He won 176 games, more than any other UI basketball coach. Bobbi "mothered" the players and provided a second home for them.

1 lb. ground beef
1 clove garlic, minced
1 Tbsp. parsley flakes
1 Tbsp. basil
1½ tsp. salt
2 cups tomatoes
2 6-oz. cans tomato paste
1 10-oz. pkg. lasagne noodles
2 12-oz. cartons large curd cream-
    style cottage cheese
2 eggs, beaten
2 tsp. salt
½ tsp. pepper
2 Tbsp. parsley flakes
½ cup Parmesan cheese
1 lb. mozzarella cheese, grated

Brown meat slowly. Add next six ingredients and simmer uncovered until thick, 45 to 60 minutes, stirring occasionally. Cook noodles until tender, drain and rinse in cold water. Combine cottage cheese with next five ingredients.

Place half the noodles in 13x9-inch baking dish; spread half of cottage cheese mixture over noodles, add half of the mozzarella and half of meat mixture. Repeat layers. Bake at 375° for about 30 minutes. Serves 6 to 8.

Tournedos Iowa

Billie Ray of Cedar Rapids and Des Moines was the first lady of Iowa for 14 years. Her husband, Robert D. Ray, served as governor of the state from 1969 to 1983 (an unprecedented five terms). He is now president and chief executive officer of Life Investors, a Cedar Rapids insurance holding company.

    2 Tbsp. butter
½ cup sliced fresh mushrooms
1 Tbsp. flour
¼ cup red wine
¼ tsp. Worcestershire sauce
¼ tsp. salt
    dash pepper
4 filets mignons
1 large ripe tomato

Melt butter and sauté mushrooms in a small saucepan. Add flour and cook slowly a few minutes, until slightly browned. Stir in wine and seasonings. Cook until thickened.

While this sauce is cooking, season and grill filets to taste. Cut tomato into four slices and grill. Arrange tomato slice on each filet and pour mushroom sauce over all.

Two-Alarm Chili

When Hayden Fry became the UI head football coach in 1979, he brought from his native Texas not only his winning ways, but also his favorite chili recipe. His wife, Shirley, shares it with us but warns it is not for the faint-hearted.

    2 lbs. coarsely ground venison or beef
1 16-oz. can tomatoes
2 cans water or 1 can water and 1 can beer
1 pkg. Wick Fowler's 2-Alarm Chili*
1 large onion, chopped
4 cloves garlic, minced

Sear meat until brown. Process tomatoes in food processor or blender for a few seconds; add to meat along with 2 cans liquid. Add all packets in Wick Fowler's seasoning except the one containing masa flour. Add onion and garlic. Cover and let simmer 1 hour and 15 minutes. Stir occasionally. Mix masa flour with enough water to make a thick but flowing mixture. Stir into chili and simmer another 15 to 20 minutes. Skim off excess grease or make ahead, chill and then remove grease that has risen to the top and hardened.

*Wick Fowler's 2-Alarm Chili is occasionally available in supermarkets. It can be ordered directly from Wick Fowler's Chili Mix, 201 East Fourth, Austin, Texas 78701.

Beef Stroganoff

Linda Glazer Toohey, Saratoga Springs, N.Y., received her B.A. and master's degrees in journalism at UI and was given the Distinguished Young Alumni Award from the University in 1979. Now vice president of trade development of the Greater Saratoga Chamber of Commerce, she formerly held executive jobs with three Gannett newspapers. Glamour magazine named her one of eleven of the Nation's Outstanding Working Women in 1979.

    1 lb. round or sirloin steak
2 Tbsp. butter or margarine
¼ tsp. garlic salt
2 10-oz. cans cream of mushroom soup
1 cup sour cream

Cut meat in 1-inch cubes. Brown cubes in butter or margarine. Season with garlic salt. After the meat is browned, pour the meat with juices into a 2-quart casserole, adding the soup and sour cream. Mix together until well blended. Bake uncovered at 325° for 2½ to 3 hours until meat is very tender. You can stir occasionally, but it's not necessary. Serves 4.

This makes a great pre- or post-game meal when served with rice or noodles. The recipe can be doubled, tripled, etc. It is quick and easy to prepare and can be made ahead and reheated.

Mexican Tamale Loaf

Mary Meis Collins, Dallas, Texas, says, "We served this as one of the main dishes for a 'Foods of the Allied Nations' supper in the Home Economics Department in 1943. We had a ball! Cooked all day and entertained family, friends and faculty guests. Dr. and Mrs. Hancher came, too."

½ lb. ground beef
2 large onions, chopped
2 cloves garlic, chopped
1 green pepper, chopped
⅓ cup oil
5 cups canned tomatoes
2 Tbsp. chili powder
1 Tbsp. salt
1½ cups yellow corn meal
1 cup whole kernel corn, drained
1 cup pitted ripe olives

Brown meat, onions, garlic and pepper in oil. Add tomatoes, chili powder and salt. Heat to boiling. Stir in corn meal slowly and cook until smooth and thick. Add corn and olives. Pour into 8-inch square baking dish. Bake at 325° about an hour. Makes 8 servings.

Wild Rice and Beef Casserole

Grace Nagle, Iowa City, volunteers in the Old Capitol Gift Shop. She served as a "gray lady" at University Hospitals for 20 years and at Mercy Hospital for 25 years.

1 cup wild rice (washed and soaked overnight)
1½ lbs. ground beef
   small onion, chopped
2 Tbsp. butter
1 4-oz. can mushrooms, drained
1 10-oz. can cream of chicken soup
1 10-oz. can cream of mushroom soup
⅓ cup top milk or cream
1 tsp. salt, or less
   dash pepper
   Worcestershire sauce
   green pepper, diced (as desired)

Boil wild rice 10-15 minutes in water to cover. Brown ground beef and onion in butter. Drain rice and combine with ground beef and rest of ingredients. Pour into casserole. Sliced almonds may be sprinkled over top. Bake at 325-350° for 1 hour. Serves 8.

Pepper Steak

Anne H. Lindblad, Iowa City, is a volunteer in the Old Capitol Gift Shop.

1 lb. round steak
2 Tbsp. oil
1 large onion, diced
1 large green pepper, diced
1 medium can tomato sauce

Cut round steak in strips and brown in oil. Put into Dutch oven the browned steak, onion, green pepper and tomato sauce. Cook on top of stove for 3 or 4 hours, until meat is tender. Serve with rice and vegetables. Serves 4.

Chili Casa Verde

Arthur Canter, Iowa City, received B.A., M.A. and Ph.D. degrees from UI. He has been a professor in the Department of Psychiatry since 1960.

3 Tbsp. oil
1 cup chopped onion
3 cloves garlic, minced
1 green pepper, chopped
2 lbs. lean ground beef
4 cups peeled and quartered fresh tomatoes
4 cups kidney beans
4 Tbsp. chili powder
1 Tbsp. vinegar
1 Tbsp. brown sugar
1 cup raisins

Sauté onion, garlic and green pepper in oil. Add beef and brown. Add remaining ingredients. Cover and simmer 1 to 2 hours or until it is as thick as you like it. Add more chili powder if you like a hotter chili.

Old Gold Trailer Park Goulash

Dolly Padilla and her husband, Don, were part of the young married group on campus just after World War II. "I used this recipe a lot during our 1½ years at the University after the war. We were dealing with small children, ration stamps and very little money, but with this recipe and a salad or fruit and cheese, we were even able to entertain once in a while." The Padillas live in Minnetonka, Minn. Don is with Padilla and Spear, a public relations firm, in Minneapolis.

    1 large onion, chopped
      bacon drippings
    1 lb. ground beef
    1 can kidney beans
    1 can tomatoes
      salt and pepper to taste

Sauté onion in bacon drippings. Add ground beef and brown. Add kidney beans and tomatoes and simmer. Add more tomatoes if mixture becomes too dry. Serves 4, but is stretchable.

Split Pea Soup

Vilda Sutherlin, Iowa City, is a docent at Old Capitol. Her husband, Bob, manages the book department of Iowa Book and Supply Company.

    1 lb. pork sausage
    1 lb. green split peas
    1 onion, chopped
    1 or 2 carrots, finely diced
    1 stalk celery, finely diced
    2 qts. water
      salt and pepper to taste

Sauté pork sausage and drain. (The fat is not used.) Rinse peas. Put sausage, peas and other ingredients in crockpot, stir and cook on low all day or on high for 2 hours and low for 4 hours. You can start with 1½ quarts water and add more later. Or, if you like a thinner soup, hot water may be added later.

Ham Loaf with Berry Glaze

Ruth Updegraff of Iowa City is a professor emeritus in the UI's Institute of Child Behavior and Development.

    1¼ lbs. precooked lean ham, ground
     ½ cup fine dry bread crumbs
     ¾ cup finely crumbled bread
     ⅓ to ½ can cream of celery soup
     1 egg, beaten and mixed with ¾ cup
         milk
     ¾ tsp. dry mustard
     3 Tbsp. finely chopped onion
     1 cup finely chopped celery
     ½ medium green pepper, chopped fine
         dash allspice
         dash ground cloves
     1 16-oz. can whole cranberry sauce

Combine ham, crumbs, soup, egg and milk, mustard, onion, celery and green pepper. Set aside. Mix allspice and cloves into cranberry sauce. Put cranberry mixture in bottom of 9x5-inch pan. Top with ham mixture. Bake at 350° for about an hour. When done, invert on platter. If it can stand a few minutes, it will cut into servings more easily.

Herbed Pork Roast

Phyllis Evans, Iowa City.

    1 4- to 6-lb. pork loin
    1 tsp. salt
    1 tsp. pepper
    1 tsp. thyme
    ½ tsp. ground nutmeg
    1 10-oz. can chicken consommé
    2 carrots, cut in cubes
    2 onions, chopped
    2 large cloves garlic, minced
    4 whole cloves
    3 bay leaves
      a few chopped celery leaves and
        parsley sprigs

Combine salt, pepper, thyme and nutmeg and rub into meat. Place in oven at 450°, uncovered, for 30 minutes. Reduce

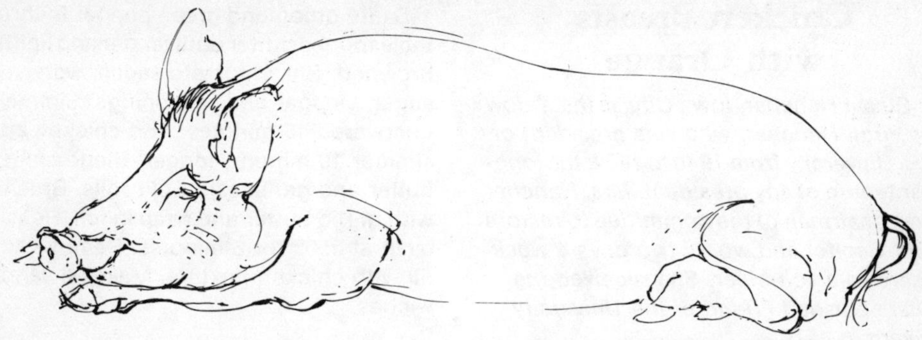

Pig, an ink drawing by Virginia A. Myers, professor of art.

heat to 350° and add mixture of remaining ingredients. Cover and bake 3 hours or until very tender. Skim fat from juices. Remove cloves and bay leaves. For gravy, blend juices and vegetables in blender until smooth. Slice meat and heat gravy before serving. Leftovers make great hot pork sandwiches.

Barbecued Pork Ribs

Eloise Z. Leinfelder of Iowa City is a volunteer in the Old Capitol Gift Shop. She received a B.S. degree in nursing and a master's degree in nursing administration from UI. During her career she was a nursing supervisor at University Hospitals, served on the faculty at the College of Nursing, was assistant chief nurse at Veterans Administration Hospital in Iowa City and was a research assistant to the director of nurses at University Hospitals.

small loin back ribs
salt and pepper
Kraft Hickory Smoked Barbecue
   Sauce
Cookie's Barbecue Sauce

Salt and pepper ribs and place in shallow pan. Bake at 350-375° for 1 hour or until brown. Remove from oven, pour off fat and cut into serving pieces. Return to pan and cover with barbecue sauces. Add water to bottom of pan to prevent scorching. Return to oven and bake for 30 minutes at 350°. Remove ribs and sauce and put in deep kettle. Marinate overnight, basting several times. Before serving, simmer in covered kettle until tender.

Gigot à la Grecque

Joyce Summerwill, coordinator of Project Art for The University of Iowa Hospitals and Clinics, brings exhibits, art education programs and performances of drama, music and dance into the hospital. Her husband, Dick, is president of Iowa State Bank and Trust Company.

 ½ **cup lemon juice, freshly squeezed**
   grated rind of 1 lemon
 3 **cloves garlic, put through press**
 2 **Tbsp. dried oregano**
 ¼ **cup finely chopped parsley**
 1 **Tbsp. coarse salt**
 1 **tsp. coarsely ground pepper**
 ¾ **cup olive oil**
 1 **6- to 7-lb. leg of lamb**

Combine lemon juice, lemon rind and garlic. Crush dried oregano in your hand or with a mortar and pestle and add to lemon juice mixture. Stir well with fork. Stir in parsley, salt and pepper. Beat in olive oil with a fork until marinade is thick and well blended.

Score the lamb all over and put, fat side up, in a large pan. Pour marinade over meat and marinate at room temperature for several hours, basting frequently.

Preheat oven to 350°. Roast lamb, basting frequently with marinade, until just done but still pink, about 1¼ to 1½ hours (12 to 14 minutes a pound). Serves 8.

"The leftover lamb is delicious served sliced and covered with Salsa Fria (relish) in steamed pita bread."

Chicken Breasts with Orange

Susan Hancher, Iowa City, is the widow of Virgil Hancher, who was president of the University from 1940 to 1964, the longest tenure of any president. Mrs. Hancher was chairman of the committee to restore Old Capitol and works two days a week there as a volunteer. She received the Distinguished Friend of the University award in 1978.

**boned chicken breasts
rosemary
thyme
sweet basil
sherry
frozen orange juice concentrate**

Put chicken breasts (any number necessary for the people you expect to serve) in baking pan. Dust breasts with rosemary, thyme and sweet basil. Cover with frozen orange concentrate (as much as is needed to cover). Add a few teaspoons of sherry. Do not salt until after cooking and only if needed. Bake for 1½ hours at 300°, basting frequently.

Chicken Pickups
(A Barbecued Sandwich)

Barbara L. Elliott of Iowa City is the wife of Chalmers "Bump" Elliott, who became Iowa's athletic director in 1970. In the ensuing years he has given Hawk fans a lot to cheer about.

**2 Tbsp. finely diced onion
2 Tbsp. finely diced green pepper
3 Tbsp. butter or margarine
2 8-oz. cans seasoned tomato sauce
¾ cup water
1 Tbsp. sugar
2 tsp. vinegar
½ tsp. salt
¼ tsp. pepper
2 cups diced cooked chicken
¼ cup melted butter or margarine
¾ tsp. garlic salt
8 hamburger buns or crisp dinner rolls**

Sauté onion and green pepper in three tablespoons butter until tender and lightly browned. Stir in tomato sauce, water, sugar, vinegar and seasonings. Simmer uncovered 10 minutes. Add chicken and simmer 10 minutes longer. Blend melted butter and garlic salt. Split rolls. Brush with garlic butter and wrap in foil. Heat in oven at 350° for 8 minutes. Remove and fill with chicken mixture. Makes 8 sandwiches.

Hong Kong Chicken

Helen Focht now volunteers as a docent in Old Capitol where she formerly worked in the dean of women's office. She was associated with UI from 1935 to 1967 and was counselor to women from 1947 to 1967. She is now retired with emeritus standing.

**3 fryer breasts, cut in 1-inch pieces
¼ cup soy sauce
1 Tbsp. sherry
1 Tbsp. sugar
1 tsp. salt
1 tsp. cornstarch
¼ tsp. garlic powder
¼ tsp. ginger
salt and pepper to taste
⅓ cup corn oil, divided
2 green peppers, cut in ½-inch pieces
1 8½-oz. can bamboo shoots
1 8½-oz. can sliced water chestnuts
2 Tbsp. honey
½ cup crushed cashews or pecans**

Mix soy sauce, sherry, sugar, cornstarch, garlic powder, ginger, salt and pepper. Add chicken and toss gently. Drain chicken, reserving liquid. Heat 2 tablespoons oil in 10-inch skillet over medium heat. Stir-fry chicken until browned, about 10 minutes. Remove; drain liquid from pan. Put remaining oil in pan, heat; stir in peppers, bamboo shoots, water chestnuts and 2 tablespoons reserved liquid. Cook uncovered until peppers are tender and crisp, 3 to 4 minutes. Add chicken; stir. Add honey and cook 2 to 3 minutes more. Add nuts just before serving. Serve with rice. Serves 6.

Chicken Babylon

Merle Miller, a student at the University in the 1930s, has written several best-selling books, including Plain Speaking, an Oral Biography of Harry S. Truman *and* Lyndon, an Oral Biography of Lyndon Baines Johnson. *Miller, who lives in Brewster, N.Y., writes: "My memories of Iowa City are warm, largely, although I do remember being menaced by Military Training which I understand is likely to be reinstated at colleges and universities. I remember winning a debate with Oxford, the English one, not the Ohio other; I remember, with affection, my stint on the* Daily Iowan, *and Smith's Cafe, which I owed a great deal of money when I left the campus abruptly. I remember many professors of political science, none in the English department. But how at my age is anyone to be sure that what I remember is true?*

"I am not much of a cook, but this Chicken Babylon, passed on by a friend from San Francisco and made in a steamer, does everything all at once and leaves a minimum of a mess."

1 4-lb. roasting chicken, cut up
flour
2 Tbsp. butter
6 green onions, chopped
salt and pepper
pinch of nutmeg
½ cup sherry
1 lb. fresh mushrooms, sliced
6 artichoke hearts
1 cup cream
chopped parsley

Lightly flour chicken and brown in butter in a large skillet. Remove chicken. Add onion and sauté until soft. Add salt, pepper, nutmeg and sherry and cook for a few minutes.

Place chicken in a large ovenproof bowl or platter that will fit inside steamer. Pour the onion mixture over the chicken and steam ½ hour. Add mushrooms and artichoke hearts. Steam 10 minutes or until done. Remove from heat; add the cream, a bit more sherry and some chopped fresh parsley. Coat the chicken with the liquid and place under broiler, if desired, to brown. Serves 6.

Cheap Chicken
(Winter Meal-in-One)

Laurence Lafore is a professor in the Department of History and author of several books, including An American Classic, *on Iowa City architecture. "This is a dish I invented myself. I make it frequently for myself (the leftover chicken is wonderful) and also for parties."*

1 chicken, cut into serving pieces
4 small white onions, peeled
4 small (or 2 large) white turnips,
peeled and thickly sliced
2 large parsnips, peeled and cut in
2x2½-inch wedges
4 stalks celery, cut in 1-inch pieces
4 medium carrots, scraped and cut in
1-inch pieces
salt

Put 2 cups water in bottom of baking pan big enough to hold chicken in one layer. Arrange vegetables in water and lay chicken pieces on top. Chicken should be mostly above water line. Sprinkle salt over all. Cover with foil. Bake 45 minutes in oven preheated to 350°.

Remove foil and baste. Cook uncovered an additional 30 minutes. It can cook about 15 minutes longer, if necessary. Chicken should be light golden brown on top, and vegetables should be tender but not soggy. With slotted spoon, remove chicken pieces and vegetables for serving. Sprinkle a little broth over them.

Put pan with remaining broth aside until cool, then refrigerate overnight or longer. Solidified chicken fat may be skimmed off and is delicious for any purpose for which butter is used. Jellied broth may be used as stock or strained for consommé.

Makes 4 servings. Can be refrigerated and reheated, but it must be covered or chicken will dry out. Best made in an oval French gratin dish, but a round wok or paella dish or any shallow baking dish of metal or Pyrex is satisfactory.

Chicken Tetrazzini

Priscilla Ann Mabie Stewart, Bradenton, Florida, teaches art history and photography at Manatee Junior College. Her father, Edward C. Mabie, was head of the Department of Speech and Dramatic Arts from 1925 to 1956. "My mother's 3x5 index card file of recipes which she exchanged with other faculty wives contains about 300 ideas for serving student afternoon teas, faculty wives' gatherings, theater and game parties, receptions and luncheons. Entertaining was a large part of 'faculty wifing' in those formal days. Daddy's students were our family, and faculty and students were Mother's concern. She loved to feed people. The recipe cards in her file, with the sources on the corner, read like a Who's Who of Iowa faculty from the 1920s to 1950s. Her card file was full of memories of Iowa. Thank you for sending me back to it."

1 3-lb. chicken
3 chicken breasts
4 Tbsp. butter or margarine
3 Tbsp. flour
1 cup light cream, warmed
1 8-oz. pkg. fine noodles or spaghetti
1 cup diced celery
2 Tbsp. minced onion
1 4-oz. can mushroom pieces, drained
3 cups canned chicken broth
2 tsp. salt
⅛ tsp. black pepper
1½ cups diced ham (optional)
1 green pepper, finely chopped
2 Tbsp. sherry
   dry bread crumbs for topping
¼ cup Parmesan cheese
   butter
   chopped fresh parsley

Simmer the chicken and chicken breasts until tender; cool, debone and dice. Melt butter or margarine in skillet, blend in flour and add cream slowly, stirring constantly until sauce is thick and smooth. Cook spaghetti according to directions on package, drain and rinse.

Combine all ingredients except topping and mix gently. Pour into 2-quart flat baking dish. Top with crumbs and Parmesan cheese; dot with butter. Bake 1 hour at 350°. Top with parsley before serving. Serves 8 to 10. Can be made ahead.

Chicken-Artichoke Casserole

Isabel Davis, Iowa City, is a 1924 graduate of UI. She was secretary and administrative assistant to the dean of the College of Education from 1926 to 1946. She has been a volunteer at the Old Capitol Gift Shop since 1976.

1 3-lb. cut-up fryer
1½ tsp. salt
¼ tsp. pepper
½ tsp. paprika
6 Tbsp. butter, divided
¼ lb. mushrooms (canned or fresh)
2 Tbsp. flour
⅔ cup chicken consommé
3 Tbsp. sherry
1 15-oz. can artichoke hearts

Salt, pepper and paprika chicken pieces. Brown in 4 tablespoons butter and put in casserole. Add remaining 2 tablespoons butter to frying pan and sauté mushrooms 5 minutes. Sprinkle flour over them and stir in consommé and sherry. While this cooks 5 minutes, arrange artichokes between chicken pieces. Pour mushroom-sherry sauce over them and bake covered at 375° for 40 minutes. May be prepared the day before.

The Tiger Hawk of the UI football team.

Chicken Thighs

Ulfert Wilke, Solon, Iowa, and Kauai, Hawaii.

**no-stick spray
chicken thighs
thyme
juice of 1 lemon
salt and white pepper
parsley, chopped**

Treat pan with no-stick spray. Sprinkle thyme on carcass side of thighs, lemon juice on skin side and salt, white pepper and lots of chopped parsley on both sides. Parsley can be cut up with scissors.

Put ¼-inch water in bottom of pan. Put the thighs in pan and broil until the parsley turns dark. Then put the pan in the oven at 350° and bake until done.

Before serving, scrape pan and spoon scrapings over each chicken thigh.

Duck in Orange Sauce

Mary Ann Colloton is married to John Colloton, director of University Hospitals and Clinics. A wing of the General Hospital has been named Colloton Pavilion in his honor.

1 4- to 5-lb. duckling
3 Tbsp. butter
1 cup orange juice
1 orange, sliced
1 tsp. dry mustard
1 tsp. paprika
½ tsp. ginger
½ cup currant jelly
½ cup brandy

Quarter duckling and remove excess bone and fat. Brown duckling in butter and place in roasting dish. Combine remaining ingredients, add to butter and simmer for 10 to 15 minutes. Pour sauce over duck. Cover. Bake 1 hour at 400°. Remove cover. Baste. Bake 30 more minutes. Sauce may be thickened with cornstarch and served with duck. Garnish with fresh orange slices and green grapes.

Paella

Eloise January, Iowa City. "This recipe, as well as the one for Gazpacho (page 55) were given to me by an excellent cook in New York who in turn learned them from her mother in their family grocery-restaurant business in Brooklyn early in the twentieth century."

12 littleneck clams
½ lb. shrimp, deveined
½ lb. scallops
1 10-oz. pkg. frozen peas
¼ cup olive oil
½ cup chopped onion
1 or 2 cloves garlic, minced
½ tsp. tarragon
½ tsp. oregano
1 cup uncooked saffron rice
1 8-oz. can Italian tomatoes
chicken broth
lobster, fresh or frozen, tails or pieces
salt and pepper
1 2-oz. can pimientos

Steam clams; drain and reserve clam juice. Boil shrimps and scallops 2 minutes; drain. Cook peas until slightly underdone. Set these ingredients aside.

In large paella pan (or skillet with cover) heat oil. Sauté onion and garlic until soft but not browned. Add herbs and rice. Stir 1 minute. Add tomatoes. Measure clam broth, adding enough chicken broth to make 1½ cups liquid. Add to rice mixture. Bring to boil; reduce heat to low, cover and simmer 20 minutes.

Add lobster and continue to simmer 5 minutes. Add shrimp, scallops and peas. Simmer another 5 minutes. Season with salt and pepper to taste. Place clams on top; cover and simmer 5 minutes more. Garnish with pimientos.

This dish can be prepared ahead of time up to the point when lobster is added.

Asparagus-Shrimp Casserole

Mary Gail Bentz of Iowa City is a volunteer in the Old Capitol Gift Shop. Her husband, Dale, is director of University Libraries.

- 1 1-lb. can green asparagus
- 24 soda crackers, crushed
- 4 hard-cooked eggs, sliced
- 1 lb. boiled shrimp
- 1 can cream of mushroom soup
- 1 cup milk
- 1 Tbsp. onion juice
- ¼ lb. Cheddar cheese, grated
- 4 Tbsp. butter or margarine

Grease casserole. Drain asparagus. Put half of cracker crumbs in bottom of casserole. Place asparagus, eggs and shrimp in layers. Mix soup with milk and onion juice and pour over layers. Top with cheese and remaining crumbs. Dot with butter. Bake 45 minutes at 325°. Remove from oven about 20 minutes before serving. Makes 8 servings.

Shrimp Casserole

Barbara W. Montgomery is a volunteer in the Old Capitol Gift Shop.

- 1 lb. fresh mushrooms
- ¼ cup butter
- 4 cups cooked shrimp
- 2 cups cooked rice
- 1 cup chopped green pepper
- 1 cup chopped onion
- ½ cup chopped celery
- ¼ cup chopped pimiento
- 1 16-oz. can tomatoes, drained
- ¾ tsp. salt
- ½ tsp. chili powder
- ½ cup butter, melted

Cook mushrooms in butter just until tender. Combine with shrimp, rice, vegetables and seasonings. Place in greased 2-quart casserole. Pour ½ cup melted butter on top. Bake in slow oven, 300°, for 50 to 60 minutes. Trim with parsley and stuffed olive slices. Serves 8.

Macaroni and Cheese Soufflé

Lois Voxman of Iowa City, a violinist, is the wife of Himie Voxman, who was director of the School of Music for 26 years. He wrote the method books for woodwinds which are used all over the world. "This is a favorite at our faculty buffets," Lois says.

- 1 cup uncooked macaroni
- 1 cup warm milk
- 2 Tbsp. butter
- 1 cup soft bread crumbs
- 3 egg yolks, slightly beaten
- 1 small onion, finely chopped
- 1 cup grated Cheddar cheese
- 3 egg whites, stiffly beaten
- 1 10-oz. can mushroom soup

Cook macaroni in salted water; drain. Add milk, butter, bread crumbs, egg yolks, onion and cheese. Fold in the stiffly beaten egg whites. Put in baking dish. Then drop by spoonfuls contents of a can of mushroom soup, undiluted, on top. Sprinkle with paprika. Bake at 350° for 45 minutes. Makes 4 large servings.

Deviled Oysters

Barbara Montgomery, Iowa City.

- 1 pt. fresh oysters, including liquid
- ¼ cup butter, melted
- 1 cup oyster cracker crumbs
- 1 medium green pepper, seeded and finely chopped
- ¼ cup finely chopped parsley
- 1 medium onion, grated
- 2 tsp. Worcestershire sauce
- 2 hard-cooked eggs, chopped
- 3 eggs, lightly beaten
- ¼ cup light cream
- ¼ tsp. dry mustard
- cayenne pepper and salt to taste

Preheat oven to 375°. Combine all ingredients and toss to mix well. Turn into 6-cup soufflé dish or casserole. Bake 30 minutes or until set and lightly browned. Nice to serve on a buffet table.

Mother's Cheese Pudding

Eleanor Pownall Simmons of Iowa City is an artist and an illustrator of books. Her husband, John, is director of The University of Iowa Press. For many years her father, the late Fred Pownall, was an associate professor of journalism at the University and director of student publications. "Homecoming weekend at the Pownalls' was almost as big as Christmas," Eleanor recalls. "So many houseguests (always bearing gifts!) that my sisters and I 'got' to sleep in the playroom. Much pre- and post-game merriment. And the inevitable, gentle deflation of Sunday morning's one last get-together before afternoon goodbyes."

  8 **slices white bread**
    soft butter
  1 **lb. Velveeta cheese, sliced**
  4 **eggs**
2½ **cups milk**
  1 **tsp. salt**
 ¼ **tsp. dry mustard**
 ½ **cup shredded Cheddar cheese**

Preheat oven to 325°. Butter generously a soufflé dish. Butter bread slices and cut in fourths at right angles, then into eighths by cutting on diagonals to each corner of the slice of bread. Layer the buttered bread pieces and the cheese slices in the dish, beginning and ending with bread.

Beat eggs, milk, salt and mustard together and pour over bread and cheese. Sprinkle shredded Cheddar over the top. Bake for 45 minutes. Serve with a blue spatterware spoon. Serves 6.

"Everybody has a version of this dish. It is the perfect antidote, at Sunday brunch, after a sporting weekend (at the stadium or arena, that is), when everyone wants something soothing and simple. Most recipes insist that it rest hours before baking. It doesn't need to; but, if you want to concoct it ahead, the fact that it *can* is a plus. You may add diced ham to it. We prefer ours, whole and warm, on the side. A fruit salad and crisp croissants would round out a restorative meal."

Illustration of her recipe by Eleanor Simmons.

Crescent Bacon Brunch

Kathy Gable is married to Dan Gable, head coach of the Hawkeye wrestling team. Under his tutelage, the Hawkeyes in 1983 won an unprecedented sixth straight NCAA championship. Dan won a gold medal in the 1972 Summer Olympics at Munich. He was head coach of the 1980 and 1984 Olympic wrestling teams.

12 **slices bacon, fried and crumbled**
 1 **8-oz. can crescent rolls**
 3 **eggs, slightly beaten**
¾ **cup milk**
 1 **Tbsp. instant minced onion**
 1 **to 2 Tbsp. chopped parsley flakes**
 3 **slices Swiss cheese, shredded**

Spread out crescent roll dough on an ungreased 14-inch pizza pan. Press the pieces together and form an edge all around the pan with the dough.

Mix the beaten eggs, milk, onion and parsley flakes together and pour onto the crescent roll dough. Sprinkle crumbled bacon and Swiss cheese on top. Bake at 425° for 18 to 20 minutes. Slice as you would pizza. Can be baked and frozen for later use.

Heavy Fried Matzoh
(Late-Night Main Dish)

Marvin Bell teaches in The University of Iowa's Writers' Workshop and has published seven books of poetry and essays. He took our request for a recipe lightly and we print his contribution in the same spirit. He writes: "Naturally, I'll retain the right to use the recipe elsewhere later on, though I'm unlikely to. I confess that writing it down for you gave me an idea for an odd prose-poem."

Four full-size crackers of matzoh
Two eggs, no shells
Some water, some margarine, some salt

Break the matzoh crackers into pieces about as big as your forefather's forefinger. Drop the pieces into a shallow bowl.

Run some cold water into the bowl. Hold a plate over the top and turn upside down to wet the pieces of cracker. Pour out the water.

Mix in two eggs, no shells.

Shovel, dump or flip it into a frying pan after melting enough margarine in the pan to coat its bottom. Spread into one layer.

Very low flame. Add margarine underneath before it sticks.

When the underside starts to brown, chop it up with a spatula and turn the pieces over. Let the underside brown again. Salt lightly in pan for effect.

Serve with cheap wine, milk or ice water.

Marvin explains further, "This is, of course, an ancient Jewish recipe, disdained by both the Czar and the Bolsheviks but successfully smuggled into America and secreted for years in apartment kitchens in the Bronx. It is not to be confused with Light Fried Matzoh, which was an attempt to imitate the Christian practice of gourmet cooking. Eating Heavy Fried Matzoh late at night should fill the diner with solid feelings of warmth and security. If there is insufficient time in which to prepare this extraordinary dish, one may achieve the same effect by swallowing a small monkey wrench. Actually, Heavy Fried Matzoh is delicious, but the most important ingredient is one's mood."

Iowa Workshop Weekday Gourmet Recipe

Novelist Gail Godwin received her M.A. and Ph.D. degrees at the University. She taught in the Writers' Workshop in 1972. Several of her novels have been published, including A Mother and Two Daughters, *a best-seller.*

1 8-oz. pkg. thin spaghetti, or fresh
    pasta if available
10 fresh mushrooms, sliced lengthwise
    butter
3 cloves garlic, finely chopped
    few sprigs parsley, chopped
    Parmesan cheese

Cook spaghetti in boiling water until "chewy-soft," about 6 minutes. Meanwhile, slice the mushrooms and sauté in butter and garlic. Combine drained spaghetti and mushroom mixture and add chopped parsley and Parmesan cheese. Serves 4 average appetites.

Macaroni Ring

Ann Mercer Feddersen, North Liberty.

1 cup elbow macaroni, cooked and
    rinsed
1 cup milk, scalded
1 cup packed fresh bread crumbs
½ cup melted butter
1 tsp. minced parsley
1 tsp. salt
½ cup grated cheese
3 eggs, slightly beaten

Prepare macaroni. Pour milk over bread crumbs. Add butter, parsley, salt, cheese and eggs. Add macaroni. Put mixture in a well-buttered ring mold. Place mold in a shallow pan of water and bake at 350° for about an hour.

Unmold. Serve with a thin sauce of creamed chicken, seafood, vegetable or cheese to pour over the macaroni mold.

Vegetables & Side Dishes

Corn Pudding

Virginia A. Myers is a professor in the School of Art and Art History and a printmaker of note.

2 eggs
1 cup milk (skim or 2% may be used)
1 tsp. cornstarch
¾ tsp. salt
¼ cup sugar
2 cups corn (frozen kernel corn preferred to canned)
butter

Beat eggs with milk until light and frothy. Dissolve cornstarch in a little milk. Add this mixture, salt and sugar to egg mixture and beat briefly. Add corn and stir. Pour into buttered 1½-quart glass or ceramic casserole. Top with a scattering of butter bits.

Place in cold oven and bake uncovered at 325° for about an hour or until mixture becomes custard-like and golden brown on top. Serves 4.

Israeli Carrots

Phyllis Evans has been a volunteer at Old Capitol ever since it became a museum. She was employed in the registrar's office for 18 years. Her late husband, Dr. Titus Evans, was head of radiation biology at UI from 1945 to 1975.

1½ lbs. carrots
4 Tbsp. butter
⅓ cup dry white wine
½ tsp. nutmeg
⅔ cup light raisins
3 Tbsp. brown sugar

Peel and cut carrots in ¼-inch slices. Put in saucepan with butter, wine and nutmeg. Cover and cook until tender. Stir in raisins and brown sugar. Continue cooking a few minutes until raisins are plump and carrots glazed. Serves 6.

Onion Casserole

Janet McNeill Bywater of Iowa City writes: "The constant flow of interesting events at The University of Iowa triggers an excuse for entertaining both local and nonresident guests, many of whom are long-time fellow alumni. This is a privilege that goes with living in Iowa City."

7 to 8 cups coarsely chopped onions
4 Tbsp. butter
½ cup uncooked rice
5 cups boiling salted water
1 cup grated Swiss cheese
⅔ cup half-and-half
1 tsp. salt

In a skillet sauté onions in the butter until transparent. Cook the rice in the boiling water in a saucepan for 5 minutes. Drain and mix with the onion. Add the cheese and half-and-half. Place in a 2½- or 3-quart casserole. Bake uncovered at 325° for 1 hour. Serves 8.

This recipe can be prepared several hours before baking. It is a hearty hot vegetable to serve with poultry, ham or beef for a buffet supper.

Sweet Potato Fluff

Florence Shea, Iowa City, says, "This has been a family favorite for over 50 years, yet I've never seen it in other recipe books nor been served it anywhere else."

3 medium sweet potatoes (or canned)
1 small banana, well beaten
⅙ cup hot cream
1 Tbsp. butter
¼ tsp. salt
marshmallows

Cook sweet potatoes, peel while hot and mash well. Add remaining ingredients and mix well. Place in baking dish. Bake at 350° for 30 minutes. Cover with marshmallows and heat until brown.

Stir-fried Green Beans and Chinese Pea Pods

Dr. Christine Grant in 1974 became the first women's athletic director at The University of Iowa. She was raised in Edinburgh, Scotland. In 1970 she received a B.A. degree from UI and in 1974 a Ph.D. degree. Her first budget of a paltry $4,000 has so increased that she now has one of the six largest budgets for women's athletics in the U.S.

5 slices bacon, chopped
1 small onion, sliced
1 lb. fresh green beans, broken into
    pieces
¼ lb. pea pods, preferably fresh
1 tsp. sugar
½ tsp. salt

Fry bacon and add onion, cooking until onion is translucent. Add beans and pea pods. Stir-fry until bright green. Add ¼ cup water, cover and simmer no more than 4 minutes. Time carefully or vegetables will be overdone. Add sugar and salt. Stir to blend and serve at once.

Variations: Broccoli can be used in place of green beans and pea pods. Torn-up romaine lettuce can be added to basic recipe after steaming.

Vegetable Casserole

Eloise January, Iowa City.

3 Tbsp. olive oil
3 Tbsp. butter or margarine
1 or more cloves garlic, chopped
3 Tbsp. chopped green onion
3 Tbsp. chopped green pepper
3 Tbsp. chopped celery and leaves
1 Tbsp. chopped parsley
3 medium yellow squash or 1 zucchini,
    sliced
3 tomatoes, peeled and chopped
1 cup sliced parboiled, rinsed okra
1 cup corn, preferably fresh
    salt and pepper
    oregano and Italian seasoning
    Parmesan cheese

Sauté garlic, onion, green pepper, celery and parsley. Add squash, tomatoes, okra, corn and seasonings. Bake in greased casserole covered for 30 to 40 minutes at 350°. Sprinkle with Parmesan cheese. Bake uncovered for 10 to 12 minutes. Serves 4 to 6.

Special Scalloped Potatoes

Arlene McBride is married to B. A. (Bunny) McBride, associate professor in the School of Art and Art History and a studio potter.

2 lbs. frozen hash browns, thawed
½ cup margarine, melted
1 tsp. salt
½ cup chopped onion
½ cup cream of chicken or cream of
    celery soup
1 cup milk
1 cup sour cream
2 cups grated Cheddar cheese
    crushed cornflakes

Combine potatoes, margarine, salt, onion, soup, milk, sour cream and grated cheese. Pour into a flat 2½-quart casserole or pan. Top with cornflakes. Bake uncovered 45 minutes at 350°.

Stoneware pitcher by B. A. McBride.

Women's rifle team, October 1936.

Brussels Sprouts Casserole

Harriet Stevens, Iowa City, has been a volunteer docent at Old Capitol since 1976. She is an assistant professor emeritus in the Department of Home Economics. The Stevens family were pioneers in Johnson County.

1 qt. (1 lb.) Brussels sprouts
2 Tbsp. butter or margarine
2 Tbsp. flour
1 cup milk
2 oz. dried beef, torn in pieces
2 oz. Cheddar cheese, shredded
3 to 4 Tbsp. chopped cashew nuts

Blanch Brussels sprouts. Melt butter or margarine in saucepan. Blend in flour. Add milk and stir. Cook until thickened. Stir dried beef and shredded cheese into white sauce.

Alternate Brussels sprouts and sauce in greased 1- to 1½-quart casserole dish. Top layer should be sauce. Sprinkle chopped cashews over top. Bake at 350° for 20 to 25 minutes. Serves 6 and can be doubled.

Good for potluck supper or luncheon.

Rice with Mushrooms

Jane Huit is a docent at Old Capitol. Her husband, M.L. Huit, was counselor to men from 1946 to 1956 and dean of students from 1956 to 1978. He is now retired. Each year the UI Teacher of the Year Award is given in his honor to the faculty member "who best characterizes Dean Huit's contribution to the university and community life."

1 cup rice
1 cup chopped tomato
1 lb. mushrooms, sliced
½ cup chopped onion
½ cup butter or margarine
3 cups chicken broth
½ cup red wine
2 tsp. salt
⅛ tsp. pepper
1 cup cooked green peas
¼ cup grated Parmesan cheese

In large skillet cook rice, tomatoes, mushrooms and onion in butter for about 10 minutes, stirring occasionally. Add broth, wine and seasonings. Mix well. Cover; simmer for about 45 minutes or until rice is tender and liquid absorbed. Stir in peas; heat. Sprinkle with cheese. Serves 6.

Spicy Noodle Casserole

Abigail Van Allen was active in raising funds for the restoration of Old Capitol and in exciting children all over the state about the project. Her husband, James Van Allen, for whom the Van Allen radiation belts are named, is head of the University's Department of Physics and Astronomy.

1 1-lb. pkg. fine egg noodles or
    vermicelli
3 cups cottage cheese
3 cups sour cream
2 cloves garlic, crushed
2 onions, minced
2 Tbsp. Worcestershire sauce
    dash liquid hot pepper seasoning
3 Tbsp. prepared horseradish
1 cup grated Parmesan cheese,
    divided
    additional sour cream, if desired

Cook noodles in boiling water until just tender. Drain well. In large bowl mix all ingredients except Parmesan cheese and additional sour cream. Add noodles and toss with two forks until well mixed. Turn into a deep 3½-quart buttered casserole. Cover and bake at 350° about 30 to 40 minutes, or until heated through. Remove cover. Sprinkle top with ¼ cup Parmesan cheese. Place under broiler and heat until cheese turns golden. To serve pass remaining cheese and sour cream to spoon over each portion. Makes 12 servings.

Excellent with any kind of roast or chicken and especially nice on a buffet table.

Spinach-Cheese Custard

Janet Van Allen is the wife of Maurice W. Van Allen, head of UI's Department of Neurology, College of Medicine. Dr. Van Allen is editor emeritus of the Archives of Neurology, a publication of the American Medical Association. Janet has recently retired as his editorial assistant.

2 10-oz. pkgs. frozen chopped spinach
    or equal amount of fresh spinach
¼ tsp. garlic salt
⅛ tsp. pepper
1½ cups (6 oz.) shredded sharp process
    American cheese, divided
¼ cup biscuit mix
4 eggs, well beaten
1 cup milk
1 Tbsp. butter or margarine

Cook frozen spinach as directed on package or chop and cook fresh spinach. Drain well. Combine spinach, garlic salt, pepper, 1 cup of the cheese and the biscuit mix. Stir in eggs and milk until well blended.

In 8-inch glass baking dish, melt butter and margarine on low burner. Tilt dish to coat bottom and sides. Pour in spinach mixture. Cook covered in oven at 325° for 20 minutes; uncover and sprinkle remainder of the cheese on top. Cook until cheese is melted. Serves 6.

Baked Pineapple Stuffing

Grace Linder, a graduate of the University, is a volunteer guide at Old Capitol.

½ cup butter or margarine
1 cup sugar
4 eggs
1 20-oz. can crushed pineapple,
    drained
6 slices white bread, preferably
    French, cubed

Beat butter, sugar and eggs until fluffy in an electric mixer. Pour over pineapple and bread and stir well. Put in a flat cake pan. Bake at 350° 45 minutes or until edges and top begin to brown nicely.

Serve as an accompaniment to ham, pork or poultry. It can be made several hours ahead and refrigerated and then baked at mealtime. Serves 6, but can be easily doubled.

Desserts

Cold Apricot Soufflé

Harriett Carpenter writes, "Wayne is from Marion and I am from Perry, both native Iowans, though we are newcomers to Iowa City (1980). It's a marvelous place to live. We've met so many talented, capable and congenial people here." Wayne has been an unofficial recruiter for the Hawkeyes for many years.

  1 cup dried apricots
1½ cups water
  ½ cup sugar
    grated peel of 1 lemon
  2 3-oz. pkgs. vanilla pudding (not instant)
  2 cups milk
  2 egg yolks
  1 envelope unflavored gelatin
  ¼ cup cold water
  2 egg whites, stiffly beaten
  1 cup heavy cream

Wash apricots. Combine with 1½ cups water, sugar and lemon peel in saucepan. Bring to boil, cover and simmer 15 minutes, or until apricots are plump and tender.

Drain syrup and add enough water to make 2 cups. Chop apricots coarsely.

Pour pudding mix into another saucepan; gradually stir in milk, apricot syrup and egg yolks. Stir over low heat until mixture bubbles and thickens.

Combine gelatin and cold water; stir into hot pudding until dissolved. Add chopped apricots. Cover and chill until pudding starts to thicken.

Fold in beaten egg whites. Whip cream and fold in. Pour mixture into 1½-quart casserole or soufflé dish. Chill until firm. Garnish with additional cooked whole dried apricots and maraschino cherries. Serves 8 to 10. Can be made a day ahead. It's a good dessert for buffet-style suppers.

Orange Bavarian Cream

Ruth Shambaugh Watkins, Clarinda, Iowa.

  1 Tbsp. unflavored gelatin
  ¼ cup cold water
  ¼ cup honey or sugar
  ¼ cup water
  1 cup fresh orange juice, unstrained
  1 Tbsp. lemon juice
  ⅔ cup heavy cream
  1 orange, divided into sections

Sprinkle the gelatin over cold water in the top of a double boiler. Let stand at room temperature for 5 to 10 minutes. Add the honey or sugar and the remaining water. Stir over boiling water until gelatin and sweetening are dissolved. Remove from heat. Add fruit juices. Set the top of the double boiler in a pan of very cold water (or chill in refrigerator) until mixture is consistency of unbeaten egg white.

Beat mixture until light. Whip cream until stiff. Fold orange mixture into cream. Pour into large mold or custard cups. Chill until set, from 2 to 4 hours. Garnish with orange sections. Sprinkle with sugar, if desired. Serves 4 or 5.

Variations: Substitute 1 cup crushed strawberries for orange juice and garnish with additional whipped cream and whole berries. You can use blueberries, raspberries, 8 stewed prunes or 12 stewed apricots and 2/3 cup juice drained from fruit in place of orange juice. Chop fruit and add with juice. Put 1 halved prune or apricot in bottom of each mold. Or substitute 1½ cups hot coffee for orange juice and use only 1/3 cup cream; add ½ teaspoon vanilla.

Strawberry Crème

Bette Thompson, Iowa City, is administrator of Old Capitol programs. She schedules use of the building, directs the volunteer program, purchases merchandise for the Gift Shop and oversees the shop.

- **2 cups vanilla wafer crumbs**
- **½ cup soft butter**
- **1 cup powdered sugar**
- **1 tsp. vanilla**
- **⅛ tsp. salt**
- **2 eggs**
- **1 pint strawberries, sliced**
- **1 cup heavy cream, whipped**

Line greased 9-inch square pan with crumbs, reserving some for top. Cream butter and gradually add sugar. Add vanilla and salt and beat until fluffy. Add eggs one at a time, beating well after each addition. Spread mixture over crumbs. Place sliced berries on top. Spread whipped cream (unsweetened) over berries. Sprinkle reserved crumbs over whipped cream and refrigerate at least 3 hours, preferably overnight. Cut in squares and top each serving with a whole berry. Serves 9.

Chocolate Cream Dessert

Kay Loeffelholz of Iowa City is a docent volunteer at Old Capitol.

- **½ cup butter or margarine**
- **1 cup powdered sugar**
- **3 eggs, separated**
- **2 squares unsweetened chocolate**
- **1 tsp. vanilla**
- **½ cup nuts**
- **18 vanilla wafers, divided**
- **1 cup heavy cream, whipped**

Cream butter, sugar and beaten egg yolks. Add melted chocolate and vanilla. Fold in beaten egg whites and nuts. Crush 12 wafers and put in bottom of greased 8-inch square pan. Add chocolate mixture. Top with whipped cream. Crush remaining 6 wafers and sprinkle over whipped cream.

Old Dental Building

Mocha-Rum Soufflé

Barbara Montgomery, Iowa City, a past president of the University Club, is a volunteer at Old Capitol. Her husband, Dr. Rex Montgomery, is associate dean for academic affairs in the College of Medicine.

- **2 envelopes unflavored gelatin**
- **1 cup sugar, divided**
- **¼ tsp. salt**
- **1 Tbsp. instant coffee powder**
- **4 eggs, separated**
- **1½ cups milk**
- **1 12-oz. pkg. semisweet chocolate pieces**
- **½ cup light rum**
- **2 cups heavy cream, whipped**
- **¼ cup chopped nuts**

In pan stir together gelatin, ½ cup sugar, salt and coffee. Beat egg yolks and milk, stir into gelatin. Add chocolate pieces and stir over low heat until chocolate is melted and gelatin dissolved. Takes 7 to 8 minutes. Remove from heat and beat with mixer to blend thoroughly. Stir in rum. Chill, stirring occasionally, until mixture mounds slightly, about 1 hour.

Beat egg whites until soft peaks form. Gradually add remaining sugar and beat until stiff but not dry. Fold gelatin mixture into egg whites and fold in whipped cream. Pour into 1½-quart dish with 3-inch oiled collar. Garnish with finely chopped nuts. When set, remove collar to serve. Serves 12.

Cheesecake

Shirley Wyrick, a sculptor, is married to Darrell Wyrick, president of The University of Iowa Foundation.

Crust:
- 1 cup graham cracker crumbs
- 3 Tbsp. sugar
- ¼ tsp. cinnamon
- 3 Tbsp. butter or margarine, melted

Filling:
- 1½ lbs. cream cheese
- ¾ cup sugar
- 3 eggs
- 1 Tbsp. lemon juice
- dash salt

Topping:
- 1 cup dairy sour cream
- 2 Tbsp. sugar
- 1 tsp. vanilla

Fruit Glaze:
- 1 cup sugar
- 2 Tbsp. cornstarch
- 1 cup fruit juice
- 2 tsp. lemon juice
- food coloring, if necessary
- fruit to make one layer

Crust: mix crumbs, sugar and cinnamon together. Blend butter with crumbs and press mixture into bottom of springform pan.

Filling: beat cheese until soft and smooth. Add sugar gradually. Add eggs, one at a time, beating well. Stir in lemon juice and salt. Pour mixture over crumb crust and bake at 375° for 30 minutes.

Topping: blend sour cream, sugar and vanilla and spread over cheesecake. Bake at 475° for 10 minutes. Cool cake and then refrigerate for several hours. Remove from refrigerator an hour before serving.

Fruit Glaze: combine sugar and cornstarch in saucepan. Add fruit juice. Bring to a boil and simmer 5 minutes, stirring constantly. Add lemon juice and food coloring, if necessary. Arrange drained whole or sliced fruit on top of baked cooled cheesecake. Use peaches, blueberries, raspberries or strawberries alone or in combination. Pour glaze over fruit. Chill until set. Serves 12 to 16.

Rehruecken

(Mock Saddle of Venison—Sweet Cake)

Vienna's loss was Iowa City's gain when Ottilie and Frederick Blodi joined the University community. Dr. Blodi is head of the Department of Ophthalmology at University Hospitals and Clinics and world renowned in his specialty. "Ottie" is a volunteer at Old Capitol.

- ½ cup sweet (unsalted) butter, at room temperature
- ⅓ cup sugar
- 3 oz. semisweet chocolate melted with 1 Tbsp. water and cooled
- 6 eggs, separated
- 1 cup finely ground unblanched almonds
- ½ cup fine white bread crumbs, preferably from homemade bread
- ⅓ cup finely cut citron (optional)
- ½ tsp. cinnamon (optional)

Chocolate Glaze:
- 3 oz. semisweet chocolate
- 3 oz. bitter chocolate
- ¼ cup powdered sugar
- 8 Tbsp. cold water
- 1 Tbsp. sweet (unsalted) butter
- slivered almonds

Beat butter and sugar until light. Add melted chocolate, egg yolks, almonds and bread crumbs. Add citron and cinnamon, if desired. Fold in stiffly beaten egg whites.

Butter a 12x4-inch loaf pan or Rehruecken form, dust with bread crumbs, shake out excess and fill with batter. Bake in a preheated oven at 350° for 25 to 30 minutes, or until cake shrinks slightly from sides of pan. Remove from oven, let cool slightly and turn onto rack for further cooling. It may fall a bit.

Chocolate Glaze: heat both chocolates, powdered sugar and cold water until chocolates are melted. Add butter, blend and pour over cake.

Decorate with slivered almonds to resemble a larded rack of venison. Serves about 10 to 12. Whipped cream may be served on the side.

Chocolate Pecan Tart

Carol Brandt of Iowa City served as chairman of the committee which produced Entertaining Arts, the Hancher Auditorium cookbook. Her husband, Dr. Berkeley Brandt, is an associate professor of surgery in the College of Medicine.

Crust:
2¼ **cups finely chopped pecans, toasted**
7 **Tbsp. firmly packed brown sugar**
6 **Tbsp. chilled butter, cut into small pieces**
1½ **Tbsp. dark rum**
Chocolate Filling:
6 **oz. semisweet chocolate**
½ **tsp. dry instant coffee**
4 **eggs, at room temperature**
1½ **Tbsp. dark rum**
1½ **tsp. vanilla**
1 **cup heavy cream**
Decoration:
1 **cup heavy cream**
3 **Tbsp. shaved semisweet chocolate**

Blend all crust ingredients together until mixture forms a ball. Press into bottom and sides of a 9-inch pie plate. Freeze for at least one hour.

Melt chocolate with instant coffee over low heat. Remove from heat and whisk in eggs, rum and vanilla until mixture is smooth. Let cool 5 minutes. Whip 1 cup heavy cream until stiff. Gently fold into chocolate mixture, blending completely. Pour into pecan crust and freeze.

About one hour before serving, transfer tart to refrigerator. Whip remaining cup heavy cream until stiff, and dollop over pie, garnishing with shaved chocolate. Serves eight.

Streusel-filled Coffeecake

Judy Richmond Brown is associated with Weeg Computing Center, The University of Iowa academic computing center, as manager of networking services. She is director of the Iowa Regional Computer Center, a computer-based consortium of liberal arts colleges in Iowa and Illinois.

1½ **cups flour**
1 **Tbsp. baking powder**
¼ **tsp. salt**
¾ **cup sugar**
¼ **cup shortening**
1 **egg, beaten**
½ **cup milk**
1 **tsp. vanilla**
Filling:
1 **cup brown sugar**
2 **Tbsp. flour**
2 **Tbsp. cinnamon**
2 **Tbsp. melted butter**
½ **cup chopped nuts**

Mix together the flour, baking powder, salt and sugar. Add the shortening and blend until mixture resembles corn meal. Add the beaten egg mixed with milk. Add the vanilla. Pour half this batter into a greased 9x9-inch pan.

Filling: mix the brown sugar, flour and cinnamon together. Blend in the melted butter, then add the nuts. Put ¾ of the filling mixture on top of batter. Pour in the other half of the batter. Sprinkle the remaining ¼ of the filling over the top. Bake at 375° for 30 to 35 minutes. It is done when a toothpick inserted into the center comes out clean. Makes nine servings.

This cake can be made ahead and frozen until needed. It is ideal for a brunch menu.

High jumper at a 1922 field meet.

Granny's Green Apple Cake

Ruth B. Evashevski of Petoskey, Mich., is married to Forest Evashevski, Iowa's head football coach from 1952 to 1960 and athletic director from 1960 to 1970. His teams were Rose Bowl champions in 1956 and 1958.

3 cups unsifted all-purpose flour
2 cups sugar
1 tsp. salt
1 tsp. baking soda
½ tsp. cinnamon
1 cup vegetable oil
½ cup milk
3 eggs
1 tsp. vanilla
3 green apples, peeled and diced
1 cup chopped walnuts
½ cup raisins
Lemon Glaze:
1 cup powdered sugar
2 Tbsp. lemon juice, or more

In large mixer bowl, blend first 9 ingredients. Beat on low 3 minutes. Fold in apples, nuts and raisins. Pour batter into greased and floured 9- or 10-inch tube pan. Bake at 350° for 1 hour and 15 minutes or until cake tester comes out clean. Cool cake in pan on wire rack 10 minutes, remove from pan and cool completely. Combine powdered sugar and juice and spoon over cake.

Steamed Persimmon Pudding

Margaret N. Keyes is a professor of home economics at The University of Iowa and director of Old Capitol. She was director of research for the 1972-76 restoration of Old Capitol and is the author of Nineteenth Century Home Architecture of Iowa City. "I received this recipe from Sybil Woodruff, former head of the Department of Home Economics. She always served this dessert at faculty Christmas parties. It has replaced pumpkin pie as my favored Thanksgiving dessert."

1 cup sugar
2 Tbsp. butter
1 cup persimmon pulp
1 cup flour
1 tsp. baking soda
½ tsp. salt
¼ tsp. nutmeg
½ tsp. cinnamon
⅛ tsp. allspice
⅔ cup chopped pecans
Pudding Sauce:
⅔ cup sugar
½ cup juice from pickled peaches
⅓ cup butter
1 egg, slightly beaten

Cream sugar and butter. Peel persimmons; put fruit through food grinder and add to sugar and butter. Sift all dry ingredients together (except nuts). Add to persimmon mixture. Add nuts. Pour into buttered, covered mold (1-pound size). Place on trivet in steamer and steam 2½ hours.

Sauce: heat all ingredients except egg in top of double boiler. When mixture is warm, add egg. Cook until thickened; serve hot on hot pudding. Top with whipped cream. Serves 8.

This dessert should be served as soon as done because it does not freeze well. It can be reheated. Be sure to use the orange California persimmons, not the wild brown ones. The California persimmons are only available from about mid-November to mid-December. However, persimmon pulp can be frozen for later use.

Indian Pudding

Cornelia Anderson Biggers of Clearwater, Florida, is a professional musician, a contrabassoon specialist who has written a book and lectured on the subject of that instrument. She plays in the Florida Gulf Coast Symphony, Tampa, Florida. Her father, William Arthur Anderson, was a professor of botany at The University of Iowa. He was on the faculty from 1931 until his death in 1949.

She writes: "I was born and educated in Iowa City. I had the whole thing—summers at the Lakeside Lab, going out to Amana for dinner and shopping, living in Woodlawn as a child, knowing Goosetown when it was really Czech, going to church at Trinity, ice-skating at City Park, playing in Clapp's orchestra, etc.

"This recipe for a hearty winter dessert comes from my mother, Ann R. Anderson, who was a librarian at the Medical Libraries at The University of Iowa."

  ⅓ **cup corn meal**
  5 **cups milk, divided**
  ⅓ **cup molasses**
  ¼ **cup sugar**
  1 **tsp. salt**
  1 **tsp. ginger**

Cook corn meal and 4 cups milk in double boiler for 20 minutes. Add all other ingredients except fifth cup of milk. Bake in greased baking dish in slow oven (325°) for three hours. At end of first two hours, stir in fifth cup of cold milk. Bake one more hour.

Serve hot with vanilla ice cream or whipped cream. Serves 4.

Lemon Dreams

Loren Hickerson is director-emeritus of Arts Center Relations at The University of Iowa. For nearly 20 years (1947-66), he held the dual posts of director of alumni records and executive director of the Alumni Association. He was a founder and first executive director of The University of Iowa Foundation. He was director of community relations from 1966 to 1972 and then director of Arts Center Relations.

For many years, Ellen and Loren Hickerson entertained the board of directors of the UI Alumni Association at annual buffet suppers at their Brown Street home in Iowa City. The suppers were features of the fall meetings of the board, usually on football weekends. Here is Ellen Hickerson's recipe for one of the favorite desserts served at those suppers.

  1 **cup flour**
  ½ **cup butter**
  ¼ **cup powdered sugar**
  3 **eggs**
  4 **Tbsp. lemon juice**
1½ **cups sugar**
  2 **tsp. grated lemon rind**
4½ **Tbsp. flour**
  ½ **tsp. baking powder**
  ¾ **cup coconut**
Frosting:
  6 **Tbsp. butter, at room temperature**
  ½ **cup powdered sugar**
  3 **Tbsp. cold water**
  3 **Tbsp. hot water**

Blend flour, butter and powdered sugar together. Press into 13x9-inch glass baking dish. Bake 15 minutes at 350°.

Beat together eggs, lemon juice, sugar and lemon rind. Add flour, baking powder and coconut. Pour over baked crust. Bake at 350° for 25 minutes, or until bottom of crust is light brown. Cool.

Frosting: in electric mixer, beat butter and powdered sugar. Add cold water, 1 tablespoon at a time. Add hot water, 1 tablespoon at a time.

Frost the cooled baked mixture and cut into squares.

Butter Bars

Susan Boyd of Chicago, Ill., is married to Willard L. Boyd, Jr., who served as president of UI from 1969 to 1981. He is now president of the Field Museum of Natural History in Chicago. While an Iowa Citian, Susan was a patient representative at the hospital. Boyd Tower of University Hospitals was named in their honor.

½ cup butter or margarine, melted and partially cooled
1 egg
1 box yellow cake mix
2 eggs
1 1-lb. pkg. powdered sugar
1 8-oz. pkg. cream cheese
salt
vanilla

Beat butter or margarine, one egg and cake mix with electric mixer until crumbly. Arrange in bottom of 13x9-inch pan. Beat two eggs, powdered sugar and cream cheese for 5 minutes. Add small amounts of salt and vanilla. Pour over cake mixture. Bake at 350° for 30 to 35 minutes or until done. Cut into bars when cool.

Chinese Noodle Cookies

Florence Shea came to Iowa City to attend the University in 1934—and never left! "I was initiated into Phi Beta Kappa in the Senate Chamber of Old Capitol. For several years I was thesis examiner in the Graduate College Office when it was in the present Gift Shop location. I have been a volunteer in the shop since 1976."

1 cup butter or margarine
½ cup sugar
1½ cups packed brown sugar
2 eggs
1½ tsp. vanilla
2 cups flour
1 tsp. baking soda
¼ tsp. salt
2 cups quick oats
1 6-oz. pkg. chocolate or butterscotch chips
2 cups Chinese noodles

Beat butter and sugars until fluffy. Beat in eggs and vanilla. Add sifted dry ingredients. Stir in oats, chips and noodles. Drop on cookie sheet 2 inches apart. Bake at 350° 12 to 15 minutes. Makes 7 to 8 dozen. These cookies freeze well.

King's Bars

Joan Overholser Houghton of Iowa City graduated from the University in 1946 and her husband, H. Clark "Bud," in 1944 (B.A.) and 1949 (J.D.). He is president of First National Bank. Their son, Steve, is coach of the University tennis team. Joan was selected for Mortar Board, a national honorary society based on scholarship and leadership.

Crust:
½ cup brown sugar
½ cup butter
1 cup flour
Filling:
1 cup brown sugar
1½ tsp. vanilla
2 Tbsp. flour
1 tsp. baking powder
½ tsp. salt
2 eggs
1 6-oz. pkg. chocolate chips

Crust: blend ingredients, mixing well. Pat dough in ungreased 13x9-inch baking pan. Bake at 350° for 10 minutes.

Filling: combine brown sugar, vanilla and dry ingredients. Beat in eggs. Pour over crust. Sprinkle with chocolate chips. Bake for 20 minutes. Makes about 32 bars and can be frozen.

Butter Thins

Eleanor Pownall Simmons grew up in a historic Iowa City house at 1602 North Dubuque Street. It was built in 1857, the year the state capital was moved from Iowa City to Des Moines. The house was once a stagecoach stop.

> 2 cups butter
> 3½ cups powdered sugar
> 5 eggs, well beaten
> 4 cups sifted flour
> 1 tsp. baking soda dissolved in ½ cup
>   sour cream
> 1 tsp. vanilla
> ¼ tsp. salt

Cream butter and powdered sugar and stir in eggs. Sift in the flour. Stir in the soda dissolved in sour cream, vanilla and salt. Mix well. Chill. Roll out very thin on a floured board and cut in shapes. Bake on a greased cookie sheet at 350° about 10 minutes. Makes about 100.

Pecan Toffee

Minnette Doderer, Iowa City, is a state representative in the Iowa Legislature. Her husband, Fred, is director of The University of Iowa Personnel Service.

> 1½ to 2 cups chopped pecans
> ½ cup butter
> ½ cup margarine
> 1½ cups brown sugar
> 1 cup chocolate chips

Sprinkle pecans in 13x9-inch pan. Combine butter, margarine and brown sugar in heavy saucepan. Bring to boil over medium heat and cook to 300° (hard crack stage), or about 10 minutes. Pour cooked mixture over pecans. Let set a few minutes. Sprinkle chocolate chips over top. Cover and let stand a few minutes. Spread melted chocolate over toffee. Cool for several hours and break into pieces.

Caramel Corn

Elsie Burton is a volunteer in the Old Capitol Gift Shop.

> 1 gallon popped corn
> 2 cups sugar
> ¼ tsp. cream of tartar
> 2 tsp. corn syrup
> 2 Tbsp. butter
> ½ cup water
> ½ tsp. baking soda

In a large pan (about 2-gallon size) mix well sugar, cream of tartar, syrup, butter and water. Cook over low heat until light brown. Do not stir but watch carefully to keep mixture from overcooking. Remove from heat and stir in soda. Working quickly, add the corn, mixing to cover well. Pour out on counter or tabletop. Can be left in small pieces or pressed into balls.

More Books

Prices include postage and handling; 1984 prices subject to change. Iowans add 4% sales tax.

On Iowa
A University and Its People
This book by mail $5.95; 2 for $10.75; 3 for $14.85.
Entertaining Arts
Menus and Recipes from Performers and Patrons Virgil M. Hancher Auditorium, The University of Iowa. Over 400 superb recipes compiled by Hancher Guild. 6 color, 20 b/w illustrations from the UI Museum of Art. Spiral bound, 6x8½". $14.70.
This Is Grant Wood Country
Compiled by Joan Liffring-Zug. 43 color, 74 b/w illustrations. 64 pages, softbound, 8½x11". $9.00
Penfield Press, 215 Brown Street
Iowa City, Iowa 52240

Inside back cover: A charming walkway is back of the Quadrangle near the hospitals and science complex.
Photograph by Esther Feske.

Back cover: Hancher Auditorium.
Photograph by Joan Liffring-Zug.